ELK HUNTING

By Jim Zumbo
North America's Top Elk-Hunting Authority

CREATIVE
PUBLISHING
international

MINNETONKA, MINNESOTA

JIM ZUMBO, an outdoor writer since the mid-1960s, has hunted elk throughout the western U.S. and Canada. Zumbo currently serves as Hunting Editor for *Outdoor Life* magazine. He lives near Cody, Wyoming, and takes joy in hunting with his wife, son and three daughters.

President / CEO: David D. Murphy
Vice President / Editorial: Patricia K. Jacobsen
Vice President / Retail Sales & Marketing: Richard M. Miller

ELK HUNTING
By Jim Zumbo

Executive Editor, Outdoor Products Group: Don Oster
Editorial Director and Project Leader: David R. Maas
Managing Editor: Jill Anderson
Editor: Steven J. Hauge
Copy Editor: Shannon Zemlicka
Creative Director: Bradley Springer
Senior Art Director: David W. Schelitzche
Art Director: Joe Fahey
Photo Researcher: Angela Hartwell
Studio Manager: Marcia Chambers
Studio Services Coordinator: Carol Osterhus
Photographer: Chuck Nields
Director, Production Services: Kim Gerber
Production Manager: Helga Thielen
Production Staff: Laura Hokkanen, Kay Swanson
Contributing Photographers: Toby Bridges, Bill Buckley/The Green Agency, Tim Christie, Cherie Cincilla/*Outdoor Life* magazine, Michael H. Francis, Donald M. Jones, Mark Kayser, Rich Kirchner/The Green Agency, Stephen W. Maas, Bill McRae, Stan Osolinski/The Green Agency, Mark Raycroft, Sil Strung, Bill Vaznis/The Green Agency, Tom Walker, Greg Vaughn/Tom Stack & Associates, Jim Zumbo
Contributing Illustrator: Cynthie Fisher

Contributing Manufacturers: Bushnell Sports Optics Worldwide – Barbara Mellman; Cabela's Inc. – Joe Arterburn, Kellie Hawkins; Carl Zeiss Optical Inc. – Karen Lutto; Crooked Horn Outfitters – Lennis Janzen; Hodgdon Powder Co., Inc. – Chris Hodgdon; Hunter's Specialties Inc. – Lori Miene; Knives of Alaska – Charles E. Allen; Modern Muzzleloading Inc. – William "Tony" Knight; Pentax Corporation – Lorri Peterson; Walker's Game Ear Inc. – Bob Walker
Contributing Agencies: Rocky Mountain Elk Foundation, *Outdoor Life* magazine
Printing: R. R. Donnelley & Sons Co.
10 9 8 7 6 5 4 3 2 1

Library of Congress Cataloging-in-Publication Data

Zumbo, Jim.
    Elk hunting / by Jim Zumbo.
        p. cm. -- (The complete hunter)
    ISBN 0-86573-126-8
    1. Elk hunting. I. Title. II. Hunting & fishing library.
Complete hunter.
    SK303.Z85 2000
    799.2'7657--dc21

                                            00-022717

Contents

Introduction

Elk hunting is a passion. It's a hunting activity not to be taken lightly, given the gear, preparation, mental attitude and physical conditioning required to make it work.

All hunters march to the sound of a different drummer. You can hunt elk the easy way, glassing slopes from the comfortable interior of your pickup truck and spending most of the day loafing in camp, or you can make a commitment and go the hard way. That often means penetrating the forest and finding the elk where they live. Or glassing and stalking, or calling, or any of the other numerous strategies. And if you're successful, your work is just about to begin. Moving several hundred pounds of meat through the forest is not fun, but it's a sobering reality if you're successful.

The history of elk management in North America is an incredibly fascinating story. The animals were shot by the millions from the time the West was discovered until the late 1800s. No one really cared, because the big animals were detrimental to livestock, farming and ranching operations, and were given little thought except for their fine-tasting flesh and ivory teeth.

But some of our early conservation-minded forefathers stepped forward, and came up with a wonderful plan to save North America's elk. From the only large remnant herd in the lower 48, elk were transplanted from Wyoming all over the West. After only 3 decades of intensive efforts, elk were introduced into the lands they once roamed, and protected from indiscriminate hunting.

Now, with almost a million elk in North America, you'd think the big animals would be easier to tie a

tag to than in the 1950s, when only a third of that number existed. But that's not the case. Averaging the harvest success rate in all the states, about 20 percent of all hunters are successful.

The bottom line is still the same. No matter how many elk inhabit our mountain country, you're still going to need to hunt hard and smart to claim one, or be extremely lucky.

This book goes into every detail of every aspect of the hunt. Whether you plan on hunting elk on your own or with an outfitter, you'll find all the pertinent details in these pages. And if you intend on calling one to

your bow in September, or hunting a giant bull during the November migration, it's here too.

Jack Atcheson Sr., a veteran Montana hunter who has hunted around the world many times over, claims that hunting elk is the toughest day in day out pursuit he's ever experienced. His thoughts are echoed by many other tough outdoorsmen who take to the slopes each year to hunt the amazing animals of our western mountains.

The pages in this book will open some of the doors that will enable you to understand what elk hunting is all about, and why it's considered to be a rough sport. But you don't need to settle for the dismal 20 percent odds. Follow along with me, and learn what it takes to be a successful elk hunter. It's all here.

Understanding Elk

Rocky Mountain bull elk

Elk Basics

Elk are said to be the most charismatic of all our big-game animals. Possessing huge antlers, these animals live in our most magnificent high mountain country, and their screaming bugles in September awe everyone who hears them.

The chocolate face and mane connect to a tan body, a lighter-colored rump, and almost black legs, making an elk a lovely sight to behold.

There are four recognized subspecies of elk. The most common is the Rocky Mountain elk (*Cervus elaphus nelsoni*), which lives in all 11 western states,

in western Canada and in isolated herds east of the Rockies. The Roosevelt elk inhabits the coastal forests of California, Washington, Oregon, British Columbia and Alaska. The Manitoba elk lives primarily in provincial and national parks in Manitoba and Saskatchewan; the Tule elk dwells only in California.

■ Rocky Mountain Elk
■ Roosevelt Elk

As members of the deer family, elk are second only to moose in size. Mature bulls commonly weigh 800 pounds or more, with the largest topping the scales

Roosevelt bull elk

cold. Excessive snow causes them to migrate to lower elevations where more food is available.

Elk breed in September and October during a much-publicized ritual where the bulls scream challenges at each other and gather as many cows as they can in harems. The typical harem averages a half dozen

Elk calf

at 1,000 pounds or higher. A Rocky Mountain bull from Wyoming had a confirmed live weight of 1,032 pounds. The Roosevelt bulls are the heaviest, with some exceptionally large animals weighing 1,100 pounds or more. The largest elk are reported to live on Afognak and one or two other Alaskan islands. Stocked there from Washington in the late 30s, there are claims of big bulls weighing 1,200 pounds.

Elk are relative newcomers to the North American continent, arriving here about 10,000 years ago during the Ice Age. It's believed the animals entered the continent by crossing Alaska's Aleutian chain of islands, which at that time were essentially a frozen land bridge.

Elk's Siberian ancestry is reflected in their preferred environments. Elk are very much at home in exceedingly cold climates, capable of withstanding sub-zero gale winds, deep snows and lengthy periods of extreme

animals, but can be much larger. I once saw a bull with 81 cows in his herd, and on many occasions I've seen large bulls with two separate harems in two widely separated areas. The bull would visit each group randomly, chasing off intruders as they appeared, and breeding cows that came into estrus.

After a 250-day gestation period, calves are typically born in May and June. Single births are common, with less than 1% of cow elk producing twins.

9

Coyotes fighting over a fresh elk kill

As members of the deer family, elk have a four-part stomach, and chew their cuds after active feeding is completed. This chewing is an important defense mechanism, allowing animals to digest their food while in the security of their beds, thus keeping exposure time in feeding areas to a minimum.

Elk antlers can grow very large on mature bulls, weighing as much as 15 pounds or more each. Yearling bulls are known as *spikes*, having single antlers averaging around 15 inches. The following year, bulls typically have a small rack that has four or five points on each antler. As the bull continues to age, antlers typically develop six points, and they increase in mass, tine length, main beam length and spread. Antlers are shed in late winter or early spring. Typically, most are gone before mid-March, but those periods may vary.

While the bulls are generally given credit as being the wariest animals in a herd, the older cows are actually the leaders. When frightened, elk commonly mill about until an old cow takes the lead and runs off. The other members of the herd usually follow in single file, with the bulls being last.

Elk have plenty of enemies, especially when they're calves. Grizzly bears are extremely adept at catching calves by coursing through birthing areas, much like a bird dog seeking a fresh scent. Black bears will often loaf around a herd of cows in the spring, waiting for an elk to have a calf, and then pounce on the calf as soon as it's born. Cow elk are also vulnerable to black bears at this time. Mountain lions are known to take full-grown six-point bulls, and wolves are extremely successful at bringing down mature bulls

as well. Recent documented cases in Yellowstone show that wolves can easily catch and kill elk almost at will, including cows, calves, and mature bulls. Coyotes may kill a calf if unprotected by its mother, especially if the calf is in a weakened condition. Cows are extremely watchful over their young; calves may remain with their mothers until they're yearlings.

Elk are very gregarious and remain in herds much of the year. In the winter, herds often combine into large bands numbering several hundred animals. Bulls often form bachelor groups in the late fall after breeding season, and remain in those groups until breeding activity begins in late summer the following year.

Cows, calves and bulls are extremely vocal; the former two communicate back and forth year round by making chirping sounds. Bulls bugle only during the breeding season, though their vocalizations are occasionally heard other times of the year.

Elk populations have exploded over the last 4 decades, and may well reach 1,000,000 in the next decade. Currently, about 800,000 roam North America. A goal in the West has been to essentially reintroduce elk into every acre of land they inhabited in the past. That objective is well on its way to being reached, and elk are being reintroduced in the East as well. Because much of the eastern habitat has been severely altered since the days of pioneer settlement, relatively few areas can support elk. Nonetheless, enthusiastic supporters and groups like the Rocky Mountain Elk Foundation (p. 123) are working hard to expand the elk's current range.

Age, Growth & Antler Development

AGE. Records indicate that elk may live to very old ages when they have nutritious feed and aren't subjected to extraordinarily severe winters. A yearling bull was ear-tagged in Wyoming in 1913, and shipped to Arizona as part of a transplant program. The bull was taken by a hunter in 1937, making it 25 years old. There are many more cases of elk attaining ages of 10 to 15 years. Of course, these are rare examples. Most bulls don't live much beyond 3 years in heavily hunted areas, primarily due to consistency in harvesting. Because cows don't have antlers and therefore aren't selectively harvested like bulls, cows are normally the oldest elk in any given herd. It's not uncommon for hunters to take cows that are 8 to 10 years old.

An elk's age cannot be determined by its antlers, though a bull with massive antlers is usually in his prime, and may be 6 years old or older. Tooth wear is the only reliable means of aging an animal, and it must be done by a qualified biologist. In some instances, wear itself cannot be used to determine age; in that case, a slice of the tooth is cut away and examined under a microscope. Old cows can often be identified by their condition—they have a darker face that shows signs of age and a blockier, more gangly body than younger cows—but these external factors are difficult to recognize unless one has observed plenty of elk.

GROWTH. Since elk are products of the habitat in which they live, their size and condition are directly related to the forage available to them. Other factors that ultimately determine an elk's size are its type (subspecies), age and the latitude in which it lives.

An interesting example regarding growth and habitat is the Tule elk of California. For years, these were known as "dwarf elk," because they attained body

ANTLER SIZE is determined by three primary factors: age, nutrition and genetics. The biggest bulls, which are typically at least 6 years old, are genetically superior animals that browse and graze on high-quality foods.

weights of only 400 to 500 pounds. Lately, however, those same elk are tipping the scales at 800 pounds and more because they've been transplanted to areas having more nutritious forage. Earlier studies were done on elk living in submarginal habitats.

Elk that live in more northerly latitudes should theoretically be bigger in body size because of a biological truism known as Bergman's Rule. Because it's colder in the North, the larger size allows less heat loss per square inch of body surface. However, elk were transplanted all over America from Wyoming herds in the early 1900s, and the evolutionary process attributed to Bergman's Rule hasn't had enough time to manifest itself. Therefore, "Yellowstone elk," as they are commonly known, are not noticeably different in size whether they come from southern Arizona or northern Montana. That's not the case with deer, which are far smaller in the

South than in the North. Likewise with moose; the biggest live in Alaska and the Yukon; the smallest live in the lower 48.

Roosevelt elk are considered to be heavier than other elk subspecies, with the largest reportedly occurring on several Alaskan islands, chiefly Afognak. Some of those bulls reach weights of almost 1,200 pounds.

Of course, the age of an elk is an important factor in its size, since older animals tend to be larger. However, very old elk may actually lose weight as they are no longer in their prime but are in a more weakened condition. Elk normally lose weight during the winter, and dominant herd bulls may lose weight during the breeding season. Elk are usually in their heaviest condition in late summer after feeding on lush foods. It may take dominant bulls several months to replace the weight they lost during the breeding season.

Raghorn bull

Spike bull

A mature bull of the Rocky Mountain subspecies is 6½ to 8½ feet long from the tip of its nose to the tip of its tail, and measures up to 5 feet at the top of the shoulder. Calves normally weigh 30 pounds when they're born, and will gain almost 2 pounds per day within 2 weeks of being born, and then 1 pound to 1½ pounds a day for the next several months. Adult cows that are on good feed may weigh as much as 550 pounds on the hoof.

ANTLER DEVELOPMENT. Male calves have no antlers the first autumn, but the following year will normally have spikes, which are single appendages that average 15 inches in length. However, some spikes may be as long as 25 inches or more. The following year, the bull is commonly called a *raghorn*, and will typically have four or five tines on each antler. As the bull continues to grow, a sixth point is added, usually in its fourth year, and the bull may maintain the six-point rack for the rest of its life. As its age increases, the bull's rack will become more massive, with longer tines and main beams each succeeding year. Many bulls develop more than six points; it's usually the older bulls that have more points, but there are exceptions to the rule.

Roosevelt and Tule elk often have somewhat of a "crown," where three points may be located at the end of each main beam. Some bulls have so-called "freak racks," with extra tines, deformed tines or bizarre growths. These are common enough that the Boone and Crockett Club now has a special category in their record book for nontypical elk.

Antlers begin growing in spring, and are covered with a protective sheath called *velvet*. It's said that antlers are among the fastest growing animal cells in the world, attaining a large mass in a relatively short period of time. By late July, most of the growth is complete. In late August, the testosterone level in the body rises to the extent where antlers stop growing and the velvet is shed, leaving almost bloody red antlers for a day or so. The antlers quickly lose their red color and take on more mahogany hues as the bull thrashes about in the brush. The tips of the tines

Mature bull shedding velvet

ROYAL BULLS have six points per antler. Hunters usually refer to the individual tines with the names shown above.

are usually white or ivory-colored, probably because the tips don't come in sufficient direct contact with foliage and bark as the bull works over the brush. Some observers of elk say the white tips are the result of bulls digging their antlers into the earth as they undergo their breeding ritual, which includes slashing trees and brush. Having studied many bulls and the angles of the various tines, I don't think that's the case.

On a typical six-point bull, the first tine near the eye is called the *brow tine*, *eyeguard* or *lifter*. The second is the *bez* or *bay*, the third the *trez* or *trey*, the fourth the *royal* or *dagger*, the fifth and sixth the *sur-royals*. Actually the sixth point is not a tine at all but the end of the main beam. A six-point bull is commonly called a *royal bull*, while a seven-pointer is called an *imperial bull*. These are descriptions coined by outdoor writers and close observers of elk. A single antler from a mature six-point bull weighs an average of 12 pounds.

A seven-point bull will raise eyebrows in most conversations, but many bulls carrying seven points on each antler do not necessarily have enormous racks.

IMPERIAL BULLS have seven points on each antler.

14

I once took an eight-by-seven, but he wasn't much bigger than the average raghorn. What's most impressive on a bull is the length of his main beam, tine length and mass.

The antlers are formidable weapons; bulls are known to kill each other in fierce battles over harems. During the rut, the antlers are constantly rubbed against saplings, often resulting in the small tree being demolished. Tines may break from the vigorous tree thrashing, or during fights with other bulls. In some areas, usually those with a high bull-to-cow ratio, broken tines are quite common.

It's not unusual to see a rut-crazed bull sporting a small tree or bush in its antlers. It's believed by some wildlife biologists that bulls may purposely carry brush aloft to intimidate other bulls.

In late winter and early spring, the testosterone level falls and antlers are shed. This often occurs on winter ranges prior to the elk ascending the mountains to their summer and fall habitats. Many times a bull will purposely knock off a single antler as soon as the first is shed, perhaps because he suddenly finds his head off balance and discards the unwelcome weight. Many matched sets of antler sheds are found lying close together.

Many antler collectors gather sheds in the spring (where legal), and sell them to buyers. Years ago, the antlers were purchased by people from the Orient and ground into powder, then used as aphrodisiacs. That practice still exists today, but most antlers are purchased by buyers who fashion them into furniture, lamps, chandeliers and other home decorations. The oriental market has switched somewhat to antlers of pen-reared elk.

The largest antler trade in the country is unquestionably in Jackson Hole, Wyoming, where antlers are gathered on the nearby National Elk Refuge by local Boy Scouts. Upwards of 10,000 elk may winter on the refuge, a good share of them branch-antlered bulls. The youngsters store the antlers until a well-publicized and highly popular auction is held, usual-

RUT-CRAZED BULLS often sport brush or saplings in their antlers. This bull, which is bugling from a wallow, still carries a fresh branch that got entangled in his antlers during rubbing.

ly in mid-May. Traders come from afar, including the Orient, to bid on the antlers. It's not uncommon for a buyer to pay up to $100,000 for a load of antlers. Early on, the scouts used the money to buy camping equipment for their troops, but nowadays the auction fetches so much money that the kids donate it to worthy causes and charities.

Elk Habitat

One of the key aspects of elk habitat is its mountainous terrain. There are exceptions, as in some high desert habitats and in lowland pinyon/juniper forests, but for the most part, elk live in steep, heavily timbered environments that are often remote with few or no roads.

A good mosaic of grassy clearings, called *parks*, adjacent to heavy forests with a nearby water source is an optimum habitat (photo above). In the summer, bulls protect their fragile velvet-encased antlers by living in more open country than usual. The rest of the year, elk are creatures of heavy forests that offer both security from predators (including humans) and shelter from the weather. Elk are seldom very far from dense cover except during the winter, when they may loaf in exposed areas.

Good habitat means good foraging. Nutritional foods produce healthy animals and hefty antlers. A mix of palatable grasses, forbs and shrubs is essential to an elk's diet, and promotes well-conditioned cows and excellent calf survival.

Roosevelt elk live in the densest timber, chiefly in steep rain forests along the West Coast. This environment may be so thick that it's virtually impossible for humans to penetrate it without a machete. The cover is characterized by a variety of evergreens including firs, cedars, hemlocks, spruces, pines and hardwoods such as red alder and maple. The undergrowth is typically composed of several species of berries, ferns, shade-tolerant saplings, devil's club and other plants capable of growing in shadowy thickets that seldom receive sunlight. Rainfall is excessive, and fog is present much of the year. The ground, fallen logs and rocks are usually layered with heavy, wet moss, making walking treacherous on steep hillsides.

Without question, this is the toughest country in which to hunt elk. The quarry is all but invisible, and most serious hunters count a day as being successful if they've so much as seen an elk. Some of the best hunting is on private land where elk aren't disturbed by many hunters and follow fairly reliable feeding patterns. Astute hunters who have access to those private lands pursue elk where their habits are fairly predictable. Large timber companies own vast tracts of land and often allow hunters to trespass on areas not being actively logged.

Several national forests along the West Coast offer public hunting. Far more hunters look for elk in clearcuts than in the dense timber because of the obvious ease in doing so.

A common hunting technique is to drive or walk to an old log landing (a large flat area overlooking a drainage where logs were gathered and stacked) before sunup and look for elk feeding in the brush. On public land, this can be extremely competitive.

Rocky Mountain elk dwell in habitats from southern New Mexico and Arizona well up into Canada, and in a few isolated places in eastern forests as well. Lodgepole and ponderosa pines, Engelmann spruce, alpine fir and Douglas fir are the primary evergreen species growing in this environment, with quaking aspen being the predominant hardwood. The farther south you travel in the Rockies, the more pinyon and juniper forests you'll see in the lowlands. In the central Rockies, quaking aspens are more common, and in the north, mixed evergreens are the norm.

Sagebrush grows in open areas adjacent to much elk habitat, forming a high desert plant community often utilized by elk in the winter. Scrub oak is common in mid-elevations, especially in Colorado, Utah, Arizona and New Mexico. Pinyon and juniper

forests grow at the lower elevations, and are characterized by arid soils, shale rock and infrequent water sources.

Old, overmature forests offer little food value to elk, since the large trees block the sunlight, preventing palatable plants from growing on the forest floor. However, these forests are extremely important as escape cover, especially in areas where hunter pressure is heavy. Extensive blowdowns composed of large trees lying on top of each other might seem impervious to any kind of wildlife travel, but elk are capable of moving within this woody tangle and use it extensively for security cover.

Forest fires and freshly logged areas engender new sprouts that elk find nourishing. Lush cover quickly takes over the burned and scarred landscape, attracting elk from hundreds of square miles. Within a decade after the disturbance, however, second growth is often so dense that visibility is virtually nil, though in some places the cover grows so slowly in old burns that elk are actually much more easily seen for many years. This occurs where the fire burns slowly, eating away all the humus layer in the forest floor and leaving a sterile base that may take decades to recover.

Elk shun human traffic areas where hunting pressure is heavy. Good habitat will have extensive areas of evergreen forests that elk can use for shelter. Those forests should be at least a half mile from a road, the farther the better. Places that are too easy to hunt and have heavy hunting pressure have few, if any, elk.

Water is a major habitat requirement. Without it, elk will be absent. In arid regions, elk will use water sources established for livestock, or a small seep that barely trickles out of the ground. Animals may also drink from large reservoirs or rivers if smaller sources aren't readily available.

If quality elk habitat has any common denominators, they're ruggedness and heavy forest. These two factors are the major reasons why many elk hunters are unsuccessful each year. Nonetheless, a biologist once told me that elk can survive very nicely on a baseball diamond, provided that the basic habitat requirements of food and water are present. To some extent this is true. Look at the many game farms where animals are contained within escape-proof fences and are essentially fed and watered daily. But those are tame elk. Their wild brethren must have a mix of necessary ingredients that cannot be man-made. The vastness, the solitude, the large chunks of escape cover and the vital foods are intricately woven together to form what we know as elk country. A creator other than man has made it, and only man can preserve it.

Food, Feeding & Digestion

Elk are popularly considered to be grazers, rather than browsers. Grazers eat grass; browsers, such as deer and moose, eat bushes, shrubs, twigs and other woody-type plants. The truth be known, elk are correctly known as herbivores and eat far more browse than people believe. A third food component called *forbs* is also an important part of their diet. Forbs include such lush plants as wild geranium, peavine and lupine. Many species of grasses are eaten, but some of the most preferred include wheatgrass, brome, bluegrass, fescue and timothy. Favorite browse plants include bitterbrush, serviceberry and ceanothus, to name a few. Food preferences for elk change with forage availability, as well as the season and location. For example, studies show that in one area in Colorado, more than 75 percent of the summer diet was grass. In Montana, 30 percent of the diet was grass; in Manitoba, 22 percent. Obviously, elk eat what is most available and what they find most palatable. Perhaps hunters categorize elk as grass eaters because hunters most often observe elk during shooting hours in grassy meadows. While animals are in the forest and during nighttime periods, however, hunters don't see them feeding on other types of forage.

Elk feeding periods vary according to the season, weather and amount of hunting pressure. Generally speaking, elk feed most actively late in the afternoon just before sundown, on and off through the night and just prior to sunrise. Animals commonly exit the forest from their beds in late afternoon and head for parks and meadows, but if hunters are present they may delay their departure from the timber until after dark. Likewise, human activity will push them from feeding areas into the forest long before shooting light in the morning. In backcountry areas or during periods where hunting season is not yet open, elk may loaf in feeding areas until sunrise and later.

Elk may feed in the timber all night and never visit the traditional open glades where you'd expect them. This may be due to the availability of sufficient nutritious feed, or an escape mechanism to avoid hunters. Forests that don't have thick overstories allow adequate sunlight to filter through the canopy and will often have plenty of grass and forbs growing in the underbrush. This is typical of some ponderosa pine forests, which often have plenty of grass growing on the forest floor, and in aspen forests whose deciduous leaves don't block the sun as much as evergreens.

Forests are classified as *old-aged* and *second growth*, and are also categorized by the tree species that inhabit them. Individual tree species are classed as *tolerant* or *intolerant*. Old-aged forests are usually very dense, with tight canopies and very little nutritional forage on the forest floor. Second-growth forests are usually the result of logging and typically have more feed, but there are exceptions.

A forest grows through a series of successional stages until it reaches the ultimate or "climax" forest. The earliest successional stages are the best producers of elk forage, while the climax forests produce the least. Typical climax forests are the spruce-fir types, which are normally very tolerant. The term "tolerance" refers to a tree's ability to live in shade. The most intolerant trees would be found in the mid-successional stages, while the most tolerant thrive in deep woods, growing very slowly in the understory until they eventually reach heights where they're dominant.

Old burns are often superb feeding spots for elk, especially within 10 years or so after the fire has occurred. The earliest plants to grow are usually very palatable, and elk thrive in these areas until the understory changes and grasses and forbs disappear. Clearcuts are also excellent feeding areas. Within a few years of a logging operation, the forest floor is typically carpeted with lush forage species, due to the beneficial effects of sunlight reaching ground that was shaded when the forest was intact.

During winter months, animals must paw through snow to find adequate forage, requiring much more time to feed. The cold weather also requires more forage than usual, which means that animals may feed well into the morning, if not on and off all day. Elk may feed on wind-swept ridges well above traditional winter ranges if enough grass is exposed by the wind.

Ivories from a bull elk (shown actual size)

As members of the deer family, elk *ruminate*, which means they have a four-part stomach and take unchewed food into the rumen, storing it there temporarily and regurgitating it later to chew it more thoroughly. This is popularly termed "chewing their cud." Once the cud is further chewed, it is processed and digested in the other three stomachs, known as the reticulum, the omasum and the abomasum.

Elk have no functional upper teeth in the front of their mouth. They ingest forage by nipping or tearing it off at the stem or just above the ground. Elk are unique in that they have one rounded canine tooth located on each side of the top of the mouth. These teeth, known also as whistlers, buglers, elk tusks or elk ivories, are prized by many hunters. In fact, the high demand for these teeth was a contributing factor in the wholesale slaughter of elk at the turn of the century. Many animals were killed just for their teeth. Both cows and bulls have ivories; the latter's are much larger. A "good" ivory is one that is well stained with a sort of bullseye marking on the bottom. These markings are the result of the primary forage species eaten by elk. I've found that ivories from elk in Idaho's Selway Wilderness are among the prettiest I've seen, no doubt because of the type of browse available in this region.

PAST AND PRESENT. Experts believe the ancestors of North American elk sported formidable tusks. Through the process of evolution, the tusks on today's elk are nothing more than small, rounded canine teeth. However, some hunters still refer to these teeth as "elk tusks."

Senses

Elk have the ability to see, smell and hear danger long before it becomes obvious. Though these animals aren't as nervous as whitetails, and don't possess the deer's fine-tuned senses, they are nonetheless quite capable of discerning trouble.

Vision is an important asset, and elk are able to see long distances. This ability is especially vital when animals are in the open. Like other big-game animals, elk have excellent night vision because their eyes are made up of far more *rods* than *cones*. The eyes of a mammal are comprised of both; the rods allow ultraviolet light to pass through, and the cones accept color. Since elk have more rods, they can see well in low-light situations, but their color perception is poor.

Unlike most other animals, elk live in bands year-round, with many pairs of eyes on the lookout for danger. It's often said that a herd will post a sentry, usually a cow, to watch for enemies. This is probably a myth, since it gives elk the ability to reason. It's more likely that females may be on guard now and then simply because cows have a maternal instinct and are accustomed to being watchful over their offspring and other members of the herd.

Elk can hear very well, though no evidence in scientific literature can pinpoint exactly how well. All things being relative, it's accurate to state that as a prey species and not a predator, an elk must intrinsically have good hearing to detect enemies. Many hunters become wistfully aware of just how good an elk's hearing is by being discovered as they try in vain to stalk silently. As mentioned in the reference to vision above, a herd of elk has many ears to warn them of danger.

An elk's sense of smell is likewise good, requiring hunters to be ever cautious of wind direction. Animals have been known to detect human scent at very long distances. On more than one occasion I've personally witnessed elk smell humans at distances greater than 1/4 mile.

It's obvious to anyone who has spent time around elk that their three warning senses are highly tuned. Since all of their senses are well-developed, elk are not usually vulnerable because of a weakness in a sense, though bulls during the rut are so focused on cows that that are less wary than at other times. Bulls may respond to and approach the sounds of hoof beats made by horses, and may trust movements and shapes that would otherwise be foreign. That's not to say that bulls are a pushover during the rut; they are simply distracted by the very powerful urge to breed.

Elk Communication

It is the bugle of the bull elk (above) that commands so much respect and awe for this animal. But the bugle is only a small part of the total vocalization behavior exhibited by elk. Bulls make other sounds besides bugles, and cows and calves make distinct sounds as well.

The *bugle* is a rut-oriented communication, occurring in September and October. It's commonly believed that bulls bugle to issue a challenge to other bulls, but that's not necessarily always the case. The bugle itself is extremely variable and lasts for a few seconds. It may start with a high or low pitch, it may be composed of three or four notes, and it may end with a series of sounds called *grunts*, *squeals* or *whines*, depending on your interpretation. The vocalization depends on the mood and status of the bull. Having observed elk in the rut for most of a lifetime, I've come up with several reasons why bulls bugle.

The first is the standard challenge issued by a herd bull as a response to another bull's challenge. The herd bull is exceedingly upset at this interloper, and may run toward him, screaming as if to say, "Come on over, pal, and make my day!" Typically, the bulls, if evenly matched, will scream at each other until they independently tear at saplings. As they slash at trees they bugle, grunt and display a most nasty temperament. This is usually a bluffing match, and does not result in a battle.

Another reason a bull bugles is to reassure the cows in his harem that he's the boss and all is well. He might be saying something like, "Stay here with me, girls, and everything will be fine." A bull usually issues this call when the cows are feeding and moving about, or otherwise acting uneasy and nervous. The bull doesn't want any of his ladies to stray away, and if his reassuring bugle doesn't work, he may lunge at them, turning the disinterested cows back into the center of his group.

When cows are trying to leave, the bull may give vent to a stern warning. This is an angry bugle, saying something like, "Get back here, ladies, or you're in big trouble."

Sometimes a herd bull bugles from his bed, almost like a sleepy yawn. Perhaps he's saying to his cows, "Everything is cool. Just leave me alone for awhile, and don't go away." During this communication, cows hardly notice the bull's bugles, and lazily continue to chew their cuds and loaf. In fact, many of the bull's vocalizations, for whatever reason, are seemingly unheeded by cows.

These are all my personal interpretations of bugles made by herd bulls with cows. Vocalizations are made by solo bulls who have no harem and would very much like some company. The loner bull often moves through the forest issuing occasional calls, perhaps saying, "Where are you, big boy. Answer me and I'm going to sneak over and steal one of your cows." Or he could simply be responding to a herd bull's challenges. He could also be calling in hopes for a response from a cow.

Bugling occurs chiefly during the breeding season when cows are in estrus. It may occur later if a cow is present that hasn't been bred the first time but comes into estrus again. It's possible to hear bulls bugle as late as November or even December.

Bulls most commonly bugle early in the morning, late in the afternoon and during the night. Many theories suggest that the bugling activity is enhanced or decreased by weather. Popular notions say that bugling increases during frosty mornings and decreases during spells of rain and warm weather. This has never been documented, but it appears accurate to say that bugling is subdued when hunting pressure is heavy and many hunters are using calls. Bulls wise up quickly, and may not bugle at all except during the night.

Nowadays, more hunters are using calls for a couple reasons. First, there are simply more hunters. Secondly, modern calls are extremely realistic and easy to use. A person doesn't have to be an expert to operate a call.

Bulls, cows and calves make a chirping sound resembling a bird call. This is often called a *mew*, because it also sounds like a kitten. These vocalizations are often referred to as *cow calls*. Calves may make a slightly higher-pitched chirp, but not necessarily.

The cow call is really a conversational utterance that is used by the herd year round, not just during the breeding season like bugling. Cows and calves talk to each other constantly, especially when they're traveling, upset or being harassed by a herd bull. The chirp is used to regroup when animals are split up, either by separated calves or herd fragments. Unknown to most people, mature bulls issue the chirping sounds too, and there's a widespread false assumption that cows and calves make it exclusively.

When bulls are actively tending cows during the rut, they make a hollow-sounding clucking noise. Few people have heard this, because you must be just scant yards away from the bull and his cows when he makes the sound in order to discern it clearly.

Cows *bark* when they're spooked. This is almost always done when they've detected danger but aren't sure of its identity. When a cow barks, she usually lifts her nose high to sort out scents, and is at full alert. The other members of the herd stare at the cow and are also at alert, but they're unsure of the problem. Usually a barking cow will not calm down, but will flee, taking the herd with her. However, she might stand rooted in one area and bark for several minutes.

Elk communication is fascinating. No words can describe the various sounds. The best way to learn elk lingo is to head for the woods and watch elk firsthand. Many national parks in the West and in Canada allow plenty of opportunities. If you can't swing that, then rent one of the many videos available. Learning elk communication will make you a far better hunter.

Breeding Behavior

Elk commonly live in large herds throughout the year, with bulls in their own bachelor groups that form in late fall after the previous year's breeding season. When their testosterone levels rise, usually in mid- to late August, bulls lose the velvet covering on their antlers and disassociate with each other. They begin actively seeking cows, trying to round up as many as possible. There is no sharing here; each bull attempts to gather a harem and breed all the cows himself.

During this period, bulls commonly thrash saplings and brush (above). This occurs extensively, with several saplings being demolished on a daily basis. This thrashing is not done to rub off the velvet, as is commonly believed. Actually, the velvet splits in long pieces and is shed quickly, with some help from the elk. Most of the velvet is gone in a day or two, and the bull then begins vigorously working on vegetation as a part of his routine breeding behavior. It's believed that during this thrashing, the bull deposits scent on the sapling from the *preorbital gland* (located near the front of the eye), either expressing his dominance to other bulls and cows or marking his territory. Bulls have been observed working over a sapling for several minutes, in some cases a half hour or longer. This practice is also responsible for the coloration of an elk's antlers.

Bull elk in wallow

Bulls visit wallows extensively during the rut. It's believed that wallowing is part of breeding behavior, since it seldom occurs much beyond October. Bulls roll in the wallow, which is usually a shallow mudhole, and cake themselves with mud. The bulls usually urinate in and around the wallow before and during their frolicking. Bugling often occurs during this activity, and bulls often thrash saplings and brush that are close by.

Wallows may be seeps or springs that are used by elk specifically for wallowing, or large waterholes also used by livestock and wildlife for drinking. Natural wallows can often be found on mountainsides where water seeps out of the ground, along moist valleys adjacent to creeks, rivers and beaver dams, or any place that water has formed. Bulls may visit wallows any time of day, but most observers

believe the visits are more frequent late in the afternoon and early evening.

The intensity of gathering cows increases as the rut advances. Bulls bugle to assert their dominance and warn off other competitors. Two evenly matched bulls may approach each other, but stop suddenly and work over a tree. Another common display is the *parallel march*, where two bulls walk rapidly or trot next to each other, resulting in one of the bulls running off. Sometimes the march is a precursor to a deadly battle in which the antlers are used in head-to-head combat. This is not one of the casual sparring matches often exhibited by bulls later in the season, but an event where the bulls are trying to kill each other. Death is not common, but may occur when a bull gives up and attempts to run away. If he stumbles or is caught in the flank by the triumphant bull, the winner may press his advance and continue to gore the downed bull incessantly until it dies. More typically, the fight ends with one or more tines being broken off by the sheer pressure of the twisting and shoving, and the retreat of the loser.

The dominant bull isn't necessarily the one with the largest antlers; it's the one that is the most aggressive. It's not unusual to see a bull with dozens of cows being avoided by a larger bull. However, since the larger-racked bulls are the oldest and most experienced, they are usually of dominant status and are successful herd bulls.

The cow remains in heat for less than a day, and if she isn't bred, will come back into heat 21 days later. The herd bull breeds each cow as she comes into estrus, all the while keeping his cows in a small

Herd bull with harem of cows

group and away from challengers. As a result, the harem master sleeps and eats little, but is constantly on guard to protect his cows. He loses weight during the breeding season, but gains it back afterward, unless an early, severe winter sets in.

As the herd bull watches over his cows, solo bulls, also known as *satellite bulls*, continually try to sneak in and breed a cow. This tactic is often successful if the herd bull is temporarily absent, chasing off another solo bull. The satellite bull runs up, quickly isolates the cow in estrus and breeds her, often unbeknownst to the herd bull. The mating event is very quick, occurring when a receptive cow stands still and allows the bull to mount her. Mating typically lasts no longer than a few seconds, culminating when the bull suddenly jerks upward and slides off. He then shows no more interest in the cow for the time being, but will be ready to breed another cow or that same one after a short rest.

Most scientific literature suggests that the cow selects the bull, preferring males with the largest antlers. However, I've seen enough cows bred by small bulls while the harem leader was gone that I don't believe that theory. I think cows that are in heat will naturally accept any available bull, since time is short during the estrus period.

When cows are being kept by bulls in a harem, they often try to escape and run off, perhaps to another bull or simply to get away. The herd bull typically dashes after the disloyal cows and herds them back to the group, similar in manner to a cow or sheep dog rounding up strays.

STAGES OF THE RUT

The breeding period has a pre- prime-, and post-rut. During much of the year, bulls remain together in

Satellite bull waiting for a chance to breed a cow

bachelor herds, but as summer progresses they split off and show an interest in cows. In the pre-rut, individual bulls engage cows for the first time, staying with them and trying to add more to their herds. Few cows, if any, are in estrus at this time. During the prime-rut, cows go in and out of heat every day, and the bull tends to them closely, never leaving except to run off a challenger. In post-rut, most cows have been bred, and bulls may wander more to look for other cows.

The rut is believed to be earlier in northern latitudes because early mating means earlier calves, thus giving them a headstart before winter begins. Theory has it that southern calves are born later since they don't face rigorous winters like their counterparts in the North.

Spike bulls often stay with their mothers until their second autumn, whereupon they're typically run off by a herd bull. Spikes are sexually mature, but do little breeding, though they're known to breed when mature bulls aren't available. Their testosterone levels are as strong as that of an older bull. If spikes aren't run off by their mothers during the breeding season, herd bulls will keep them away. The small bulls often remain at the outskirts of the herd, just far enough away to avoid rousing the ire of the herd bull. After the rut, spikes may return to their mothers, remaining with the herd until the following spring when they develop into branch-antlered bulls.

Cows do not breed as calves, but come into estrus the following autumn as yearlings. Twinning is extremely rare; most cows bear single calves. Some cows seem to have a mind of their own when the herd bull tries to keep them in a group. Single cows or small groups may wander off to join another herd, even though it is lorded over by a less dominant bull. There are many mysteries regarding elk behavior, many of which may never be sufficiently answered.

ANTLER BATTLES between mature bulls are violent affairs. Typically, the fight begins as the bulls crash into each other with full force (top). The antlers are then twisted back and forth as each bull tries to throw the other off balance (center). The fight ends when one bull concedes (bottom) and is chased off.

Movement Patterns

Elk are great nomads, often wandering great distances between summer and winter range. Herds in the northern latitudes travel far more than those in the South because of climate. Elk in much of Arizona and New Mexico, for example, migrate little where snowfall is light because they have adequate feed to sustain them on a year-round basis. Roosevelt elk in coastal forests may migrate very short distances or not at all. In more extreme parts of their range, however, elk must migrate from summer ranges to wintering areas because deep snows blanket their food (above). Elk also migrate because of seasonal food availability as they seek more palatable forage, even in milder climates. These movements may amount to only a few miles or so, but are discernable. To a lesser degree, elk may move because of insects. Hunter pressure is also a factor in moving elk from one area to another, and even though elk may travel long distances when disturbed, studies show they often don't establish effective escape cover strategies in unfamiliar country. This displacement makes them somewhat more vulnerable.

Migrations due to extreme weather begin as soon as enough snow accumulates to move elk. Research shows that elk may travel comfortably in 3 feet of soft, powdery snow, but with difficulty in crusted snow that's 2 feet deep. The distance covered during migration varies with the length of the route, the weather and human disturbance factors. Elk in the northern Yellowstone area are known to migrate up to 80 miles. Daily distances traveled by elk may average a dozen miles or more, depending on external factors and time of year. Tagging studies indicate some amazing movements. In one study, a cow elk and her calf were seen in one area in June; 2½ months later they were observed 110 miles away.

When migrating, elk often use the same trails year after year. Many of these routes are made to circumvent human development such as highways, buildings, bridges, etc. If disturbed while migrating, elk may select a different route, usually returning to the original one at some later point.

Though elk typically return to critical winter ranges year after year, some do not complete the journey, but linger on high ridges where persistent winds sweep the snow away from forage. Bulls are most often willing to remain at higher elevations. The best-known elk wintering range is at the National

Elk Refuge in Jackson, Wyoming. Upwards of 10,000 elk may winter there each year.

Elk movements may be somewhat dramatic during hunting season because of human disturbance. Several studies prove conclusively that elk move away from roads and trails, seeking refuge in secure cover anywhere from ½ to 2 miles or more from the nearest disturbance.

Daily movements revolve around feeding and bedding areas. Elk may travel over 2 miles to feeding areas from bed locations, depending on the suitability and availability of bedding cover. Animals normally begin walking to their bedding areas at first light, lingering somewhat if they aren't pressured by humans or predators. It may take 1 or 2 hours for elk to ultimately reach the bedding areas. Animals seldom bed in the same places day after day, but normally remain in the same general area.

Conversely, elk leave their beds in late afternoon and begin the trek to feeding areas. They may actually run briskly to a meadow as soon as they leave the forest, dropping their heads and eating as if they hadn't had a meal for weeks. If elk aren't disturbed by humans, they may approach the meadows when the sun is still up, but they normally wait until almost dark to enter openings, and almost always after dark if hunters are about.

Bedded bull elk

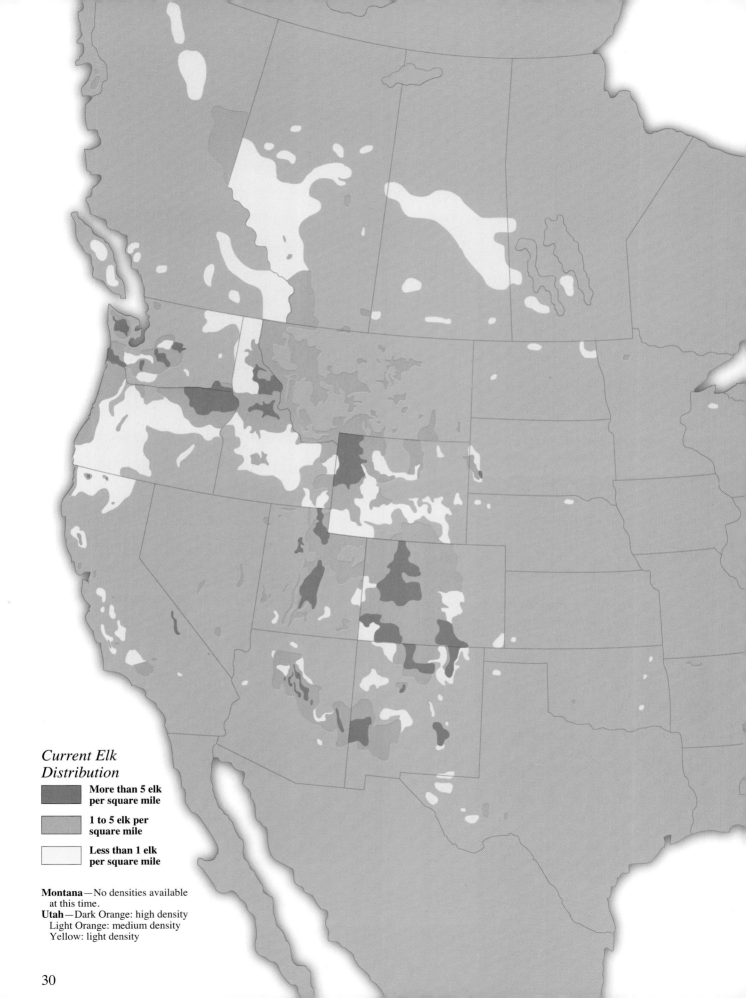

*Current Elk
Distribution*

**More than 5 elk
per square mile**

**1 to 5 elk per
square mile**

**Less than 1 elk
per square mile**

Montana—No densities available
at this time.
Utah—Dark Orange: high density
Light Orange: medium density
Yellow: light density

Elk Populations

Anyone familiar with elk is aware of their incredible success story. When our shores were first visited by Europeans, about 10 million elk lived in North America. Because of unlimited hunting, those huge numbers dropped to less than 50,000 at the turn of the 20th century. Now, thanks to conservation practices and wise management, it's estimated that 1 million elk will inhabit this continent in the near future.

Though elk are found in many states from coast to coast, 95 percent of them live in nine western states (Arizona, Colorado, Idaho, Montana, New Mexico, Oregon, Utah, Washington and Wyoming). Of the four subspecies, the Rocky Mountain elk is by far the most numerous, living in all the western states, Canada and many eastern states. The Roosevelt elk lives in the west coast states, including Alaska, and British Columbia. The Tule elk inhabits only California, and the Manitoba elk dwells in Canada.

Of the typical western elk states, four have the lion's share of elk—Colorado, Wyoming, Montana and Idaho. Colorado alone is inhabited by more than one-fourth of the elk in North America— about 225,000. Utah is rapidly gaining status as a major elk state in the Rockies. Oregon is the leader for elk numbers out of the Rocky Mountain region, with animals ranging from the rain forests of the West Coast to the arid juniper country of the high desert in the central region.

Some ambitious transplant programs have accounted for well-established herds in the east. Arkansas held its first elk hunt in 1999, and more than 700 elk were stocked in Kentucky at the turn of the 21st century.

These are unquestionably the "good old days" of elk hunting; for more than 150 years it's never been better.

Historical Elk Distribution circa 1500s
(Range shown in dark green)

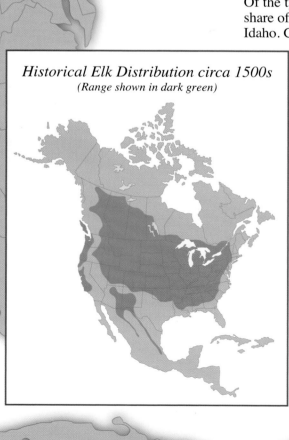

Maps and elk population information from *Status of Elk in North America, 1975-1995*, which was compiled by S. Dwight Bunnell and produced by the Rocky Mountain Elk Foundation, P.O. Box 8249, Missoula, MT 59807-8249.

Elk-Hunting Equipment

The author and his reliable Winchester Model 70

Rifles & Ammunition

Newcomers to elk hunting are usually faced with the dilemma of selecting an adequate firearm. Because elk are so much larger than deer, novice hunters are often intimidated by an elk's size and believe that only a big-bore magnum will get the job done. Deer hunters who use rifles commonly want a larger-caliber rifle than they have; hunters who pursue deer in shotgun-only states are often in a quandary as to where to start.

Any discussion of firearms for elk must, in my opinion, address the extreme shot—the one that is imper-

fect but attainable. Of course, no hunter should ever take an iffy shot that has a low percentage of success because of the chance of wounding the quarry. But there are many opportunities for a killing shot when the animal isn't standing broadside for the optimum shot. The bullet might need the wherewithal to penetrate a great deal of tissue and massive bone before hitting the vital area.

CALIBERS FOR ELK

If an elk cooperates, you can put it down quickly with a .243, or even one of the centerfire .22 caliber rifles. But that shot must be placed with absolute precision. It's far better to use a firearm with enough energy that will get the job done under all circumstances. Then too, some states have minimum restrictions on caliber size.

An acquaintance of mine used a .22/250 when he had cow tags. This caliber, by the way, is illegal in many states, and is most popularly known as medicine for prairie dogs and woodchucks. My friend killed three cows with that rifle, all of them shot in the ear. He never fired unless he had a solid rest and the animal presented the perfect shot. I would never recommend that anyone use a caliber of this nature for elk, even where it's legal, and I don't condone my friend's actions. Frankly, my opinion is that if a person wants to challenge himself by using the lightest rifle he can get away with, then he might consider small-game hunting. Going light applies nicely to fishing, not to hunting. Unlike fishing, hunting is a consumptive sport. There is no catch-and-release; once you squeeze the trigger and put the quarry down, you have an animal or bird in your hand or on the ground. And because we use a deadly force to possess that animal, we want to do everything humanely possible to cause no suffering. The best way to accomplish that objective is to use a firearm that has sufficient energy to put an elk down instantly or nearly so.

Another acquaintance of mine uses a .243 for elk. He's a skilled woodsman, and says he has never lost an animal, always waiting for a perfect shot. Again, I don't agree with that mindset, but in the hands of a marksman who patiently waits for the correct target, a small caliber will effectively take down an elk.

Jack O'Connor, the legendary shooting writer, was a champion of the .270 for elk. He took many bulls with that caliber, but it must be remembered that many of O'Connor's hunts were guided affairs in wilderness areas where he had good shots at standing bulls. O'Connor was a superb shooter, and could pinpoint the bullet directly into the elk's lungs at great distances.

Then there was Elmer Keith, another famous gun writer who was of the school that the biggest bores were best. Keith loved the .375 H&H, the .416 Rigby, and other heavy-duty firearms. If it was up to Keith, no elk hunter would be afield with anything less than a .338 Mag.

Today, most hunters are faced with shots at elk running through brush, or standing in dense vegetation, or otherwise offering a difficult target. The light .270 bullet, or one of similar caliber, may not have the energy to punch through the intervening material in order to ultimately reach the vitals. Nonetheless, the .270 remains popular among elk hunters and should be rightfully considered as one of the top elk calibers available.

I've taken four elk with a .270, two bulls and two cows. The bulls and one cow were hit behind the shoulder; the other cow was shot in the head. The latter cow went down instantly, and the other three animals ran an average of 80 yards.

Every discussion about firearms must include the very obvious and very mandatory subject of bullet placement. As in the case of the two aforementioned hunters who use a .22/250 and .243, the sole objective is precision shooting. When those three elk were struck by my .270 bullet, the lungs were impacted, and the goal of a humane kill was accomplished.

However, I know of several elk that were hit with .270's but unrecovered because the bullet did not penetrate through to the vitals. In most cases, they struck the shoulder bone (right) and were either deflected or stopped. The conclusion here is that a bigger bullet with more energy would have punched through the bone and struck the vitals.

Heart-lung area

PROPER SHOT PLACEMENT is an important consideration regardless of what game animal you hunt. On an elk, your best shot is always the heart-lung area.

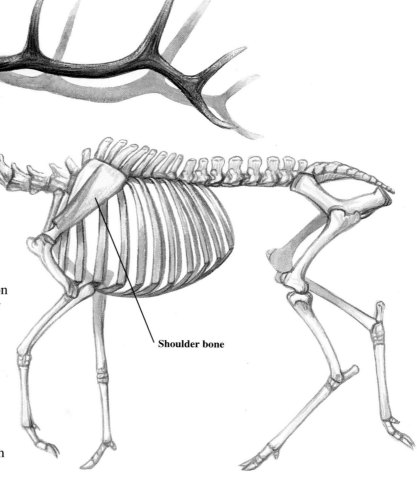

Shoulder bone

The .30/06 and 7mm Remington Mag are perhaps the most widely used calibers, according to informal surveys I take in my seminars. I believe this is so because they produce adequate foot-pounds of energy but don't deliver a punishing recoil like that of bigger bores. Then too, people tend to form opinions on products, whether they're vehicles, beer or washing machines. Because those two calibers are written about widely and are the favorites of many gun writers, hunters no doubt often choose calibers based on what they read.

My first big-game rifle was a Winchester Model 70 Featherweight .30/06. It was a college graduation present, and I was told to go to the local sporting goods store and pick out the gun of my choice. Being an avid Jack O'Connor reader, I had my heart set on a .270, but none were in stock. A .30/06 mounted with a 4X Weaver scope caught my eye, and it became my favorite big-game rifle for more than 20 years. In those days, elk were few in number where I lived, so I broke the rifle in on mule deer. All in all, I took 19 bull elk with that Winchester, and it's still very much in use, though my son hunts with it these days.

That rifle was like an old friend. I knew exactly where it shot at various distances, and I had the utmost confidence in its capabilities. I asked a lot of it at times, though I never exceeded its limitations. I knew the cause of practically every scratch and nick on the stock, and I wasn't the least bit embarrassed by of its unsightly appearance.

For the last 10 years I've used a variety of rifles, but seem to favor a Browning A-bolt in 7mm Rem Mag. Like the .30/06, this rifle fits me well and I have plenty of confidence in it.

.30/06 Cartridges

The firearm is topped with a 3X9 scope, but I usually leave it at four power, which I've become accustomed to after years of looking through my old Weaver 4X.

The Browning is flat-shooting, and packs a wallop downrange. I've had some folks scoff at the 7mm, calling it a glorified .270, but when the chips are down, this gun performs beautifully. I've taken a number of elk out to 350 yards, as well as plenty of other game, including several moose, bears and African game.

It's important to remember that a firearm is a tool. Just as a carpenter prefers a particular hammer because he likes the way it balances and swings, so does a hunter become attached to a gun. The smooth feel of the rifle as it is brought to the shoulder, the familiar pull of the trigger and the comfortable slide of the bolt are all components of the gun's personality, so to speak. This confidence and fondness for a rifle manifests itself when you're in the woods. It's a terrible feeling to have a negative attitude toward a rifle. If you feel good about a gun, you'll hit well with it.

Hunters who want heavy payloads often choose the .300 Win Mag and .338 Win Mag. Both these calibers are seen far more commonly in the elk woods these days, and are the choice of many whitetail hunters who want a different gun for elk. A good number of the Weatherbys are also seen in the elk woods, especially the .300.

Many hunters planning their first elk hunt ask me what caliber to buy, and my reaction is always the same. If that person lives in a state where rifle hunting is allowed, I suggest they bring out their deer rifle, provided it's at least .270 caliber. For hunters who live in states where only shotguns are allowed for deer hunting, I recommend any rifle, again a .270 or better. In either case, I insist that hunters fine-tune their rifles at the range and shoot them as much as possible. Ideally, it's a good idea to shoot varmints with the rifle to be used for the elk hunt because of the practical field experience. Since you'll be shooting at various distances and from various positions, this is great practice.

Some people are most unhappy with the noise and recoil of the bigger bores. For example, if your heart is set on a .338 because you've heard good things about it, go out to the range with a pal who has one and shoot it. You may decide this is not the gun for you, and you won't have invested money on a firearm that you really don't like.

Thanks to modern technology, recoil can now be tamed with one of the many muzzle brake systems available today, but the downside is more noise. A compromise is possible by using ear protection while hunting. I strongly recommend Walker's Game Ear (below), which does double duty by allowing you to hear subtle woodland noises but also blocks out loud sounds that could damage your ears.

It's a mistake to bring one of the so-called "brush busters" on an elk hunt, such as the .30/30 Win, .35 Rem, or .444 Marlin, even if you expect to hunt in heavy timber. The old belief that these calibers plow through brush has been disproven, and their poor trajectories have no place in elk country. You never know where a long shot might be necessary.

To determine how your rifle and bullets perform, check a ballistics table. Each bullet has its own characteristics because of varying weight and design.

The tables show velocity expressed in feet per second, and energy expressed in foot-pounds. Most elk hunters prefer a bullet to deliver at least 1,800 foot-pounds of energy at the point of impact. Note that lighter calibers may retain velocity for long yardages, but the energy drops off rapidly.

MAKING THE SHOT

Expect fairly long-range shooting on an elk hunt, far more than you're accustomed to in the whitetail woods. A 300-yard shot in the West may be average in some areas. Don't make the common mistake of trying to judge distance if you have little experience in open country. Chances are excellent that you'll overestimate yardage every time. At 300 yards an elk looks like a mouse, and gravity will be doing nasty things to your bullet. Be familiar with your gun's performance, and use one of the new laser rangefinders to help you determine distance.

A common error among newcomers is to sight in their rifles at urban ranges around home that have only 100 yard targets. When the hunter is faced with a shot at an elk that's 300 or 350 yards, he has no idea where his bullet will end up. Trajectory tables are helpful, of course, but there's no substitute for actual practice. If you can, go to a farmer's field (with permission, of course), and test your rifle at long distances. Better yet, as I already mentioned, shoot some woodchucks or other varmints. When you practice, check your rifle to be sure the scope is adjusted properly, and then shoot at different ranges, with varying positions. Try them all—prone, standing, kneeling and sitting.

A sling is a must for carrying the rifle over your shoulder, especially since you're apt to be in broken country and may need both hands free to keep your balance and help you get around in the woods. A sling is also useful in helping you steady the rifle if

you must make an offhand shot. Buy a sling with a wide part where it rides on your shoulder for the most comfort. Some slings also have special material that doesn't slip.

Always carry some sort of rifle rest, since you may find yourself in a location where a fairly long shot is necessary and you have no natural rest. I use 36-inch Underwood shooting sticks, which are designed for kneeling or sitting shots. They are held together with a shock cord and break down into 12-inch sections that fit in a belt holster. But I carry the sticks extended as an aid when I'm walking in rugged country. That way, the sticks are in my hand, and I don't have to fish them out of the holster and make extra noise to set them up.

A bipod permanently attached to the rifle works well, but I don't particularly care for them because they affect the gun's balance and snag underbrush. It's my opinion that they are unattractive, and look like something used on the front battle line.

Walker's Game Ear

The Game Ear is a hearing enhancement and safety device developed for hunters. The lightweight device amplifies high-frequency sounds, such as an elk bugling in the distance. It also contains a safety circuit that protects your hearing from sounds greater than 110 decibels, such as a muzzle blast.

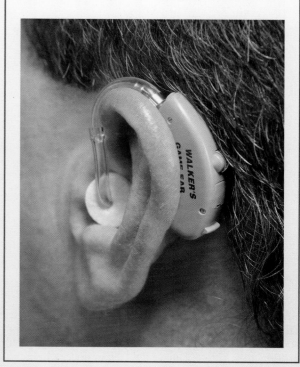

The distance at which you zero-in your scope is a subject of some debate. Some hunters sight dead-on at 100 yards; some like to group their bullets at 3 inches high at 100. Whatever you do, be sure you remember where your rifle is hitting, especially if you own several guns and zero them in differently. I prefer sighting in dead-on at 100, because I don't have to think where my gun is zeroed when a bull shows up and my brain isn't working at its best. That's often a problem with people who own several guns and zero them in differently or constantly change the zero on one gun during different trips.

Ammunition is the subject of endless debates. Some elk hunters use a bullet weighing 150 grains, and some wouldn't be seen with anything less than a 180-grain projectile. Handloaders have some very definite parameters, and those who buy factory loads at a sporting goods store are less discriminating. It's safe to say that there are eight or so major ammo manufacturers in the U.S., and that no popular sporting round of adequate weight is unsuitable for elk. Some offer more penetration than others, and some have different explosive designs. One thing that's agreed upon by all is to use the same bullet at practice as those you'll use hunting, since different bullets perform in a varying manner in the same firearm.

Don't leave home without a good scope on your rifle, unless you are keenly adept at using an open-sighted gun. Scopes are invaluable at helping you pinpoint the precise target area at a distance, and

TYPE OF CARTRIDGE	ENERGY (in foot-pounds) AND TRAJECTORY (in inches above (+) or below (-) line of aim)							
	100 Yards		200 Yards		300 Yards		400 Yards	
	Energy	Trajectory	Energy	Trajectory	Energy	Trajectory	Energy	Trajectory
.243 Winchester* (100 grain)	1615	+1.6	1332	0.0	1089	-7.5	882	-22.1
.270 Winchester (150 grain)	2343	+1.7	2021	0.0	1734	-7.5	1480	-21.6
7mm Remington Magnum (160 grain)	2511	+1.7	2097	0.0	1739	-6.9	1430	-19.8
.30/30 Winchester* (170 grain)	1355	+1.8	989	-4.6	720	-24.5	535	-62.6
.30/06 Springfield (180 grain)	2522	+2.0	2174	0.0	1864	-8.4	1590	-24.3
.300 Winchester Magnum (180 grain)	2967	+1.6	2501	0.0	2094	-7.2	1741	-21.0
.338 Winchester Magnum (210 grain)	3157	+1.8	2653	0.0	2214	-7.9	1834	-23.2
.375 H&H Magnum (270 grain)	3510	+2.2	2812	0.0	2228	-9.7	1747	-28.7

BALLISTICS TABLES help you to determine the effective killing range of your cartridge and bullet drop at various ranges. This table lists the energy in foot-pounds at ranges from 100 to 400 yards. As a rule, use a cartridge with at least 1,800 foot-pounds for elk. Trajectory figures show how far the bullet strikes above (+) or below (-) the point of aim at ranges from 100 to 400 yards. *Note: Due to the lack of energy in both the .243 and .30/30, these cartridges are not recommended for elk.

TARGET SHOOTING your rifle at distances over 100 yards is the best way to be prepared for a long shot at an elk.

help you see the quarry in poor light or weather. Be absolutely sure the scope you use is waterproof. The last thing you want is to see the bull of your dreams standing before you, but your scope is fogged. A scope with good light-gathering ability will help you see the quarry far better in low light.

Many hunters prefer to use variable powered scopes these days, with 3X9 unquestionably the most popular. It's never a good idea to change powers in the field if a variable scope is used. Instead, stay with the power you used during practice sessions. In most situations, four or five power is optimum. In fact, many hunters prefer a single-power scope, especially the four power. Scope caps are useful in keeping snow, rain and moisture off the lenses. Be sure you use caps that are instantly removable. You don't want to be fussing with them when an elk presents a fleeting shot.

The type of action to use on your rifle is a matter of personal preference. My own is a bolt-action; I wouldn't think of using anything different. Perhaps that stems back to my early notions on western hunting when most folks were changing over from lever-action carbines to bolt-actions. This system is almost infallible, and is easy to clean and disassemble. It's also an extremely strong and reliable action.

Pumps, lever-actions, single shots and semi-autos are also seen in the elk woods, but my observation is

that semi-autos are the most popular next to bolt-actions. I'm not a fan of the semi-auto because I'm a firm believer of Murphy's Law, which states that if a gun can jam, it will. I've seen countless semis jam at inopportune times, and many elk lost because of those failures. On the other hand, I know many hunters who are pleased as punch with their semi-autos and wouldn't part with them for anything. An inherent danger in using a semi-auto is the idea that you'll have a quick second shot (and more) if necessary. That notion leads to hurrying up the first and most important shot, or making that first shot a careless one. Regardless of the action, every hunter should be of the mindset that only one shot will be necessary.

Is there the perfect elk rifle, a "10" that is far and away the gun that beats them all? I think not. We can all argue the merits of our rifles until we're blue in the face, discussing ammo choices, actions, scopes and all the accessories that go with them. But the bottom line is always the same, and is best summed up by my Montana outfitter buddy Billy Stockton, who simply says, "Shoot whatever you want, as long as you can shoot it." You can take those words to the bank.

Muzzleloading

Muzzleloading rifles are rapidly gaining popularity in the elk woods. Recognizing this boom in hunting interest, many states have established exclusive seasons for muzzleloader hunters, and in some units, only muzzleloaders can be used.

The most obvious and unique feature of the muzzleloader is its ability to fire only one shot. If another shot is urgently required, a lengthy process is required to reload the firearm, compared to the quick action of a centerfire rifle. Perhaps it's this challenge that endears it to many hunters, as well as the awful ballistics (compared to a centerfire rifle) that require the shooter to get close to the target.

MUZZLELOADER TYPES

There are two basic types of muzzleloaders, the flintlock and caplock. The former has an external firing system requiring a flint hammer to strike steel, thus producing sparks that ignite a small quantity of powder. The explosion sends heat through a flash hole, igniting the major powder charge behind the projectile. The caplock has a percussion cap that sits on a nipple. When the hammer strikes the cap, which contains an explosive fulminate of mercury, the resulting flame sends heat through the nipple and the flash hole, and touches off the major charge in the barrel.

In 1985, a new concept in caplocks, called in-lines, became popular. The inventor, William (Tony) Knight, wanted a muzzleloader that was more reliable, more accurate and lighter in weight than traditional caplocks. On an in-line, all the firing components—striker, cap, nipple, flash hole and powder—are positioned in a straight line. Tony's latest invention, the Knight Disc™ rifle, takes in-lines one step further by using shotgun primers instead of traditional percussion caps for unsurpassed dependability.

The most popular propellants used in muzzleloaders are black powder and Pyrodex, though there are a few others. Pyrodex seems to be the choice of most muzzleloader hunters because it's more stable and safer, than black powder and doesn't foul the bore as much. Black powder is graded from FFFFg, the finest, down to Fg, the coarsest. The fine grade is used in flintlock pans, and Fg is generally used in shotguns. For elk hunters, FFg is most commonly used. Pyrodex is available in several grades, but the RS type is recommended for large-caliber muzzleloaders. Lately, Pyrodex pellets have become available. These are cylinders of a specific grain measurement (50-grain pellets are most popular) that are simply popped down the muzzle, eliminating the need to measure and pour loose powder.

Pyrodex pellets

A standard load for most hunters, regardless of the powder, is around 100 grains, but it's a good idea to test the firearm with different loads to check performance. Before you begin tinkering with powder charges, become familiar with the firearm manufacturer's recommendations. Many hunters carry *quickloads*, which are cylindrical tubes that accommodate the properly measured powder and projectile for one shot. This eliminates the need to search for a second projectile and measure powder.

Calibers come in a variety of sizes, but elk hunters should use either .50- or .54-caliber rifles. There is only $4/100$ of an inch difference between the two, but the .54 accommodates heavier projectiles.

The round ball, conical bullet and sabot are the three basic projectile choices. As far as performance goes, the round ball is worst, the sabot the best. Though the round ball can be very accurate at short ranges, its trajectory is inferior to the other two.

QUICKLOADS carry a single projectile and a pre-measured powder charge.

Standard round ball weights are 180 grains in .50 caliber and 215 grains in .54 caliber. Conical bullets range from 385 grains in .50 caliber to 425 grains in .54 caliber. The sabot, which is simply a bullet encased in a plastic sleeve, ranges from 180 grains to 325 grains.

The muzzleloading projectile is positioned over the powder charge with a ramrod, which is carried under the barrel. To start the bullet initially, a tool called a *short start* helps push the projectile in; then the ramrod is used to complete the process.

Cleaning a muzzleloader involves taking the gun apart to remove the black powder or Pyrodex residue. Upon reassembly, you need to apply the appropriate lubricating oils. Between shots, it's a good idea to run a patch down the bore. Of course, in hunting situations, a quick second shot may not allow time to employ a cleaning patch.

Knight MK-85 Predator in-line muzzleloader

Hunters often use telescopic sights on muzzleloaders. Though controversial in some circles because the sight detracts from the "tradition" of black powder hunting, supporters claim the scope allows a more accurate shot, and therefore fewer animals are wounded.

There is a certain amount of polarization regarding muzzleloader hunters. On one side are the traditionalists who use the original-style guns, black powder, round patched balls and accessories that are more reminiscent of the old days. Many of them wear frontier-style clothing and are interested in nostalgia and accouterments of a bygone era. On the other side are the so-called modern shooters, most of whom shoot in-line rifles, Pyrodex powder and some sort of bullet rather than a round ball. Their garb is more often modern camo than mountain man attire.

I started off with a flintlock some 35 years ago. I was highly skeptical of the gun because I had no experience with it and no mentor to teach me how to shoot it. I secured the gun to a tree and tied a string to the trigger when I tried it for its maiden first shot. When I jerked on the string and the smoke and flame cleared, I realized that perhaps it would be safe to fire it. I began practicing with a light load and built my way up to a standard charge.

Later I bought a traditional caplock rifle, and then a few more, and finally got into in-lines. I find the entire aspect of muzzleloading not only fun, but effective. I like the idea of escaping the competition in the elk woods during general season hunts by being able to hunt with a muzzleloader during an exclusive season.

Before hunting elk with a muzzleloader, be sure to check regulations carefully. Some states have minimum caliber requirements, and some prohibit sabot bullets and telescopic sights.

Muzzleloading Misadventures

I've had plenty of experiences in the elk woods, some good, some not so good. Some were caused by the firearms, others by Murphy's Law.

Once, I had climbed up a ridge after hiking 2 miles in the rain and waited near a saddle with plenty of fresh elk sign. A bunch of cows drifted by, and I was distracted watching them when I sensed the presence of something else in the other direction. I turned to see a big bull standing broadside at 40 yards. I slowly raised my muzzleloader, placed the sight behind the front shoulder and gently squeezed the trigger. I couldn't believe what happened next. The cap exploded, but the main charge didn't ignite until what seemed like an eternity later. When the gun went off, I fired under the bull's belly.

I couldn't believe it. I had experienced a "hangfire," a lapse between explosion of the cap and the ignition of the powder behind the bullet due to damp weather. Evidently, when the cap went off and there was no immediate bang, my brain wanted the projectile to go out so badly that I pushed the gun just slightly forward, thus lowering the point of aim. At least that's what I think happened. Whatever the case, the bull walked off unscathed, and would you believe he stopped 80 yards away and stared at me? I was in full camo, shaded in a small thicket, and the wind was in my favor. I tried to very slowly reload the gun and almost had the chore accomplished, but the bull barked at me and ran off toward his cows.

Obviously, wet weather—rain or snow—is the enemy of any muzzleloader. Take steps to keep the percussion caps and powder dry in inclement weather.

Another time I saw a bunch of cows running full speed down a sparsely timbered slope. Realizing I could cut them off if I acted quickly, I sprinted up a game trail and got down on one knee. The herd ran by 60 yards away, and I waited for a bull to show up, if indeed one was trailing the cows. He was, a big five-pointer, and just as he crossed the trail I was on I gave a shrill bark on my cow call. The bull stopped on a dime and looked at me. I was ready, with my gun already firmly sitting on my shooting rest, and I squeezed the trigger. I was thinking "meat on the table" and walked through the thick cloud of smoke to look for my bull. He wasn't there, which was perfectly natural, since most elk will run off a ways before expiring. I'd just follow the blood trail and walk him down. But there was no blood, which was still okay, because sometimes there's little if any blood at the spot the animal was hit. I'd just look harder, find blood and carefully dog his trail. Still no blood, so I began making ever-widening circles.

An hour passed and still no elk. I was dumbfounded. There was no way I could have missed that bull. I had a steady rest, and my muzzleloader was dead-on.

I went to the very spot I shot from and pinpointed the place where the bull was standing when I shot. For the first time I noted that he had stood behind a light screening of oak brush, and I was suddenly struck with the depressing thought that perhaps the bullet had been deflected by a branch. I walked straight into the brush, on the same path the projectile would have taken, and saw a sight that made me want to cry. The bullet had centered a 1-inch-thick branch that had gone unnoticed when I was drawing a bead on the big bull. The bullet also ripped into another branch behind the first, and I could see by its line of travel that it was badly deflected. Obviously I had seen only the bull and not the vegetation in between us.

Bowhunting

The vocalizing nature of elk make them a perfect quarry for bowhunters. Archery seasons are held during the rut, allowing hunters to call elk to the bow. Another section in this book describes calling technique in general (p. 88), but bowhunters have unique considerations. Along with the need to get close, the hunter must have shooting lanes—a difficult task in dense forests. When the elk approaches, it might suddenly appear, giving the hunter little opportunity to stealthily draw the string.

Then too, bowhunters normally don't have the advantage of watching from a treestand. The elk hunter must be mobile and physically fit, usually hiking to the elk over very rough terrain.

All the major elk states have exclusive September bow seasons, and some have later seasons as well, especially for antlerless animals. Because those early seasons are held during warm weather, special consideration of the meat is necessary. Since their seasons are the first to be held, bowhunters have the advantage of pursuing unhunted elk. Elk are also vulnerable due to their heightened aggressiveness during the rut, and the silence of the bow doesn't spook animals out of the country as firearms might.

HARVESTING an elk with a bow is one of archery's greatest accomplishments.

ARCHERY EQUIPMENT FOR ELK

Just a few decades ago, bowhunters were rare in North America. The longbow was used exclusively, and when the recurve bow appeared on the scene, championed by the late, infamous Fred Bear, the sport suddenly erupted. Not long afterward, the compound bow gained popularity, and today the vast majority of bowhunters use the compound.

The advantage of the compound is its *let-off* ability, which reduces the draw weight at full draw by 50 to as much as 80 percent. What this means is that you can draw the string, and have the relief of dramatically reducing the strain in holding the string back at full draw. For example, a compound bow with a 60-pound draw weight and a 80-percent let-off enables the shooter to hold only 12 pounds at full draw. Translated in a hunting scenario, let's say you've called in a bull and he's just 1 yard from your shooting lane, but he's temporarily thrashing a sapling. You can pull the bowstring back and hold it comfortably until the bull walks into the opening. This is impossible to do for any length of time with a longbow or recurve. The compound also shoots an arrow faster, so it has less drop and more energy at the strike zone.

There are dozens of compound models these days, each having their unique system of cams and pulleys. The limbs are most commonly made of molded or laminated fiberglass.

When you purchase your bow, it's wise to do so from an archery dealer, since clerks are experienced and make wise recommendations. You can also be measured for your proper draw length, and learn how to adjust the draw weight to your ability. Many archery stores have practice ranges inside or outside the stores, giving you a hands-on experience. This can be an an invaluable assist if you're new to the sport. It's critical to match your bow to your physique and capability. The draw length must fit you precisely, or you won't be able to anchor correctly. If the draw weight is wrong for you, you might wear yourself out and shoot poorly if it's too heavy. If too light, your arrow may not have sufficient energy to penetrate to the vitals.

Longbows are by far the most difficult to shoot. Some traditionalists make their own or buy wooden bows. Recurves, usually made of laminated wood and fiberglass, have double-flexed limbs and deliver more energy than longbows.

Bowsights are immensely popular with compound shooters these days, with new models and concepts appearing on the scene each year. The typical sight is mounted just above the arrow rest and has several pins, which are usually set at 10- or 15-yard increments. The archer looks through a peep sight in the string when at full draw, and then lines up the correct pin on the target. Archers who dislike sights shoot instinctively, lining up the target with their eye and arrow. This is, of course, the most challenging, and it demands constant practice.

Like bows, arrows have come a long way in the last couple decades and vary widely. Two basic elements do not vary, however. These are the absolute need to be straight and uniform—exact in weight, length and diameter.

Carbon and aluminum are the most popular, but some hunters still shoot fiberglass and wood arrows. Invest in high-grade arrows that are properly spined and are suited to your bow.

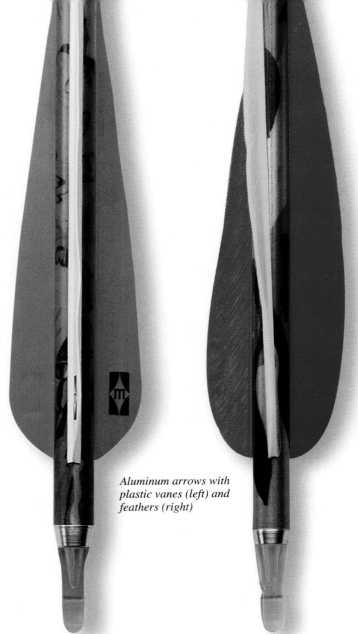

Aluminum arrows with plastic vanes (left) and feathers (right)

The fletching, once made exclusively of feathers, is now made of feathers or plastic, depending on the preference of the hunter. Fletching stabilizes the arrow and helps it rotate, which is essential for accuracy and a suitable trajectory. The nock at the end of an arrow should be securely fastened, and it's a wise idea to have brightly colored fletching and nocks. You'll be able to see the arrow easier as it hits the target, and you'll locate a spent arrow afterward with less searching.

Broadheads must be in perfect working order to accomplish their mission. They should be matched to your arrows, and they must be exceedingly sharp. You can choose from dozen of styles, some having two, three, or more blades, some with detachable blades, different shaped blades, etc. Take a blade sharpener on your hunt or extra replaceable blades,

Broadhead with replaceable blades

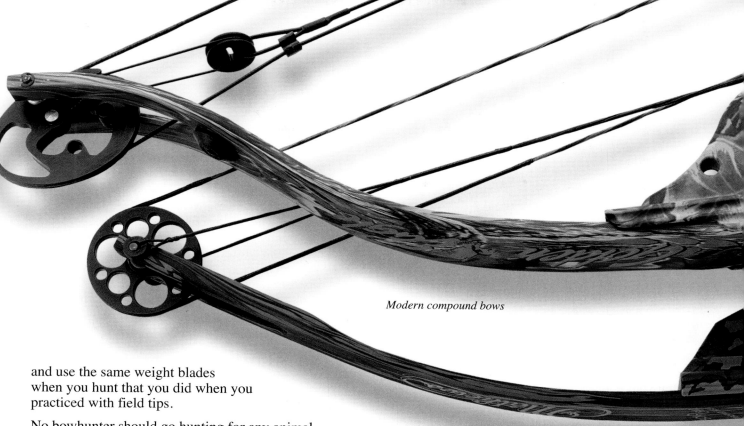

Modern compound bows

and use the same weight blades when you hunt that you did when you practiced with field tips.

No bowhunter should go hunting for any animal without spending extensive time at the practice range. Of all the hunting choices today, bowhunting requires the most practice. And though an elk is big and more difficult to miss than a deer, his very size requires a pinpoint shot, since hitting the very large shoulder bone is woefully ineffective. A neck shot is also unwise. There is only one target on an elk that the bowhunter should take, and that's directly behind the shoulder and into the lungs. To do this, the bull should be standing broadside in an opening wide enough for your arrow to clear without striking the tiniest twig. Any other shot is iffy, unwise and unethical.

It goes without saying that knowledge of calling, with both the bull and cow call, is extremely important because of the necessity of luring the quarry in close.

Because elk can't be counted on to use trails as consistently as whitetails due to the vast country they live in, hunting from a treestand is impractical. Calling is essentially the best option, though bowhunters may be able to ambush elk near water holes in arid areas and during dry

DEDICATED PRACTICE is mandatory for anyone planning on hunting elk with a bow and arrow.

spells. Wallows are other places to watch from a stand, and can be extremely productive. Elk that go to wallows and are undisturbed can often be readily patterned.

Full camo clothing is a must for bowhunters. Most people have a decided preference for a particular pattern of camo. Whatever type you like, the important rule is to remain motionless, since an elk will spot movement from a distance. Make your draw when the animal is moving behind brush or is momentarily distracted. Face paint or a tight-fitting face mask should be worn, as well as camo gloves. Keep in mind that an elk might be well within range, but because of brush or the animal's angle you won't have a shot. You'll need to wait him out, and hope your camo and the wind keep him fooled to the point where he'll take a step and finally offer a shot.

If that happens and your arrow is true, you will have experienced one of the finest moments in bowhunting. Working a bull one-on-one, from the ground, is one of bowhunting's greatest challenges.

Hunting Optics

Optics are necessary tools if one is to be a consistently successful elk hunter. Long-distance glassing is almost always possible; it requires good binoculars and a spotting scope, though many hunters don't use the latter. Binoculars are also indispensable in timber, where they'll help to identify an elk in the brush, or distinguish antlers on a partially obscured bull.

BINOCULARS. There are literally hundreds of models of binoculars on the market today, some made in the U.S., some in Europe and some in the Orient. With this vast variety, it's not difficult to choose one that meets your expectations and is within your budget.

It's always a good idea to get a hands-on look at binoculars before you purchase them. Try several at a sporting goods store, checking them for clarity, ease of focus, fit, weight and other details. Be cautious of glasses made by obscure companies, and be sure to look at the warranty.

There are two basic types of binoculars, porro prism and roof prism. The porro has an offset profile of both tubes, while the roof has straight tubes. The roof prism eliminates the offset housing, decreasing bulk and weight and offering a new design to the market. Basic binoculars, regardless of the style, have a pair of prismatic-erecting telescopes that appear as one when placed to the eyes. The twin binocular tubes are connected by a hinge so they can be adjusted to fit different eyes. Most binoculars have some sort of eyepiece device to allow eyeglass wearers to look squarely into the tubes. The standard design is a simple rubber ring or cup that can be rolled in or out, depending on the need.

Binoculars are classified by two sets of figures, such as 7X35, 8X42, etc. The first figure is the magnifying power; the second refers to the diameter of the objective lens (in millimeters). The objective lens is the one farthest from the eye; the ocular lens is closest. When looking through different binoculars, you may notice that the higher the magnification, the more difficult it is to hold the

Zeiss 8x30 Classic binoculars

binoculars steady so the image doesn't waver. For this reason, when using high-magnification binoculars it's always best to rest your elbows or forearms on a solid object.

Be certain that your binoculars are waterproof, have good light-gathering ability and are lightweight, since you'll be doing plenty of climbing. Heavy binoculars can literally become a pain in the neck, and cause serious aches. A number of manufacturers offer a harness (right) that keeps the glasses tight to your chest, preventing them from bouncing around and whacking you when you move suddenly.

SPOTTING SCOPES are merely telescopes constructed to take a beating. Not many years ago, they were heavy and bulky, and few hunters bothered to carry them. New models are light, compact and easy to stow in a daypack along with a small collapsible tripod. Hunters who are looking for a special bull, or are hunting where there's a minimum number of tines for a bull to be legal, generally use a spotting scope.

A spotting scope may have a single magnification lens, or a zoom with multi-power capability. The 20-power single lens is popular among hunters who don't care about additional magnification. Zoom lenses vary widely, such as the 15X45 or the 25X50. To help protect them, some scopes have rubber or heavy plastic coatings. A tripod is a must when using a spotting scope, especially one with a high-magnification lens.

I'm a firm believer in binoculars as well as spotting scopes. It surprises me how many elk hunters I see afield who don't carry binoculars. As far as I'm concerned, they're a must for safety's sake, because you'll need them to identify a suspicious form or movement in the brush. Of course, a rifle scope should never be used for that purpose, though some hunters rely on them. That's not only a bad idea, but dangerous if the movement turns out to be another hunter.

I can't remember how many times binoculars have helped me spot elk that simply could not be seen with the naked eye, even animals feeding somewhat in the open but mixed in with patches of brush. I suspect that hardly a hunt goes by when binoculars didn't point out a elk in the distance or even up close.

A spotting scope has become more of a permanent fixture in my daypack these days, primarily because I've become more of a believer in its value under practically all circumstances, and also because the modern versions are easier to carry.

One of my favorite strategies is to get up on a ridge before daylight and set up my spotting scope. As it gets light enough to see, I use my binoculars first and slowly scan every chunk of ground I can see. If

BINOCULAR HARNESS STRAPS, like this model from Crooked Horn Outfitters, are a better option than a simple neck strap because they keep the binoculars tight against your chest when you're not glassing.

nothing turns up, I go to my spotting scope and view areas farther away. Obviously, you can see far more detail with the spotting scope than you can with binoculars.

Many states now have regulations requiring hunters to take bulls with a specific antler configuration. In some units, only spikes are allowed, and in others, a legal bull must have four points on each side. Binoculars are vital in determining points, but a spotting scope does the job far better. Many times a spike can't be identified from a bunch of cows in the distance, and though practically every branch-

antlered bull has at least four points, you can never be sure if it's legal until you make a positive identification. A spotting scope resolves the dilemma.

Trophy hunters who want to closely examine a distant bull's antlers use a high-quality spotting scope. In this case, simply counting points isn't the objective—the hunter wants to be able to estimate tine length, mass, beam length and width.

During very hot days, heat waves distort the sight picture in a spotting scope; the higher the magnification, the more severe the waves. There isn't much to be done to resolve this problem, though most elk are spotted early in the morning and late in the afternoon when the air temperature is cooler.

RIFLE SCOPES are by far more popular than open-sights in elk country, and in fact, I can't remember the last time I saw someone using an open-sighted rifle on an elk hunt. There are literally hundreds of

models of scopes on the market today, though half a dozen domestic companies and three or four foreign countries produce the bulk of them.

A scope has one purpose: it magnifies the target so the shooter can accurately place the bullet. I learned recently it has yet another purpose, one that isn't obvious until your eyes change with a bit of aging. Because many of us must use bifocals, the ability to peer down a gun barrel and line up a front and rear sight is not a good option anymore. The scope presents a flat rather than 3-D effect, enabling us to simply line up the crosshairs at the intended target.

Scopes may be fixed, as the 4-power, or variable, as in the eminently popular 3X9. My personal opinion is that the 4- or 5-power is adequate for any situation. The higher magnifications decrease the field of view and increase waver. Also, moving animals are always harder to find at high magnifications.

Several criteria should be considered when you buy a scope. I like a crisp focus, and I want a scope that is absolutely waterproof. The latter is exceedingly important, because a fogged scope is a useless scope. The last thing a hunter needs is to look through a scope and not see the target.

The reticule is a matter of personal preference. I personally like the dot in the crosshairs, while some hunters prefer the post, or other designs. What I don't like is a scope that has high-tech compensators that tell you bullet drop at different distances, as well as scopes with built in rangefinders to determine distance. I don't believe you should have to think very hard when you line up on an animal. A hunter's brain is already working overtime at the imminent prospect of a shot—no sense complicating the procedure by trying to figure the scope's technicalities. Too often the shot is quick. There isn't much time to react and consider all the things you need to know to use the scope properly. I think it's far better to use a simple, basic scope, know the ballistics of your gun and bullet and take your shot using the proper hold for the distance involved.

Another optics tool, and one new to the industry, is the laser rangefinger. Now produced by several companies, this device accurately reads the distance in yards and displays it with a digital printout. Depending on the model, you can accurately determine distances up to 800 yards. The laser rangefinder is about the size of standard binoculars, very light, and has twin tubes on one end and a single tube on the other.

There has been some discussion lately about the pros and cons of high-tech hunting gear. The laser rangefinder has been mentioned by some hunters as an example of equipment that's gone too far in the way of technology. I believe that we may have gone too far with some hunting products, but any tool—like the laser rangefinder—that helps a hunter make a more accurate shot and reduces the chance of wounding an animal is welcome.

"I Won't Need My Binoculars"

There's an interesting myth regarding binoculars when people hunt brushy country or forests with dense undergrowth. Many believe that the tight cover doesn't require any kind of visual assistance, and binoculars aren't needed.

I had an experience years ago that taught me a good lesson. I was living in Utah at the time, and hadn't gotten an elk so far during the season. My son Dan, who was about 12, wanted to go elk hunting with me, and only 1 day in the season remained. I had plenty of work to do around the house, and I had just about given up getting an elk because of the tremendous hunting pressure on the public land we hunted. Nonetheless, Dan was anxious to tag along one more time, so we left the house in the dark and I followed the usual line of pickups into the mountains. I had no idea where to go, because the area had been hammered during the 2-week season. As far as I was concerned, every living, breathing bull that survived the onslaught had to be either on private land or high up in the primitive area.

I settled on a spot where some pals said they'd seen elk tracks near a waterhole, which incidentally was just 75 yards from the main road. As far as I was concerned, those elk were on the moon. I had no expectations of seeing them. Dan and I hiked up on a cedar bluff cov-ered with fairly thick cedar trees, and eased through the vegetation as quietly as we could. I was stunned when we jumped a cow and calf. There actually were some live elk on the mountain.

Ten minutes later I saw a sight that brought me to full attention. I had just walked past a tree and spotted an elk bedded under a very thick cedar. I had only a bull tag, and couldn't identify its sex, though it was light colored, as a bull would be.

I reached for my binoculars, but they weren't there. In my haste to leave the house in the morning, and since I hadn't planned on hunting that day, I'd left them at home.

The elk and I had a long staring contest. I raised my rifle ever so slightly and looked over its head with my 4-power scope. The branches were so thick I couldn't identify antlers, but I knew I was handicapped with the scope. I lowered the rifle, not taking my eyes off the elk, and raised it again, trying with all my might to see antlers. Still no dice, though I was almost positive I could see the bases of his antlers and a brow tine. Still I waited, hoping he'd turn his head ever so slightly, betraying the antlers that I was convinced were atop his head.

It was not to be. Suddenly the elk leaped up and bounded over the edge of the knoll. At that very moment my rifle was just off my shoulder and when I snapped it back the elk was gone. I ran hard for the knoll and caught my boot in the rocks, spraining my ankle. The physical pain wasn't bad at all compared to the mental anguish of watching a bull with enormous antlers run out of sight.

There's no doubt in my mind that binoculars would have allowed me to absolutely identify the giant bull, and I went home dejected and thoroughly disgusted with myself for leaving the binoculars at home.

Accessories

You'll need far more gear when you hunt elk than with most other big-game species, because of the very basic need to literally process the carcass in the woods—unless you're lucky and can drive to it with your vehicle. Unfortunately, that doesn't happen very often.

Fanny packs carry a limited amount of gear, and are generally too small to accommodate your needs, though some oversized models store an amazing amount of gear. The advantage of the fanny pack is the ability to carry items around your waist and avoid using your back if you have a back problem.

A daypack (opposite page) carries far more hunting equipment. Be sure the pack fits well and is carried properly on your shoulders. The straps should be wide and well-adjusted, and a waist strap should fit snugly to keep the pack snugged into your back so it won't bounce. Avoid packs made of materials that are noisy, and be sure your pack is thoroughly waterproof; otherwise everything you carry will be soaked during storms. Many packs have all sorts of straps and strings attached. Eliminate the ones you don't need, since they can be noisy and distracting. If the state you're hunting requires hunter orange, buy a hunter orange daypack. In fact, you may want to do it anyway, regardless of the law, for safety's sake.

If you might be faced with the option of backpacking boned meat, several garbage bags will serve as a liner to keep blood from soiling the pack's contents. Never place warm meat in plastic bags; be sure the meat is well cooled first—otherwise it sours in a matter of a couple of hours.

If you plan on packing whole quarters, consider a convertible-type pack that transforms into a pack-frame, or a pack with an oversized pocket to accommodate the quarter.

A very sharp knife is essential, along with a sharpener. If you intend to bone the elk, take along an extra knife, one with a long, slender, flexible blade. A fish fillet knife works well. This tool allows you to cut away meat from curved bones, sliding the blade along and cutting into hard-to-reach places. Many hunters use rubber gloves nowadays to protect themselves from any diseases or parasites the carcass might be harboring.

A saw is mandatory if you plan on quartering your elk by sawing down the backbone and across the spine. There are all sorts of saws; the best have a long flexible blade with a stout handle. Some saws are small enough to be carried on a belt holster. As a rule of thumb, the bigger, heftier saws are far better than small ones, simply because you can apply more pressure and the bigger blade is more effective. Most saws come in belt holsters that are carried around your waist, eliminating weight and bulk in your backpack.

Rope is always handy, and may be essential if you need to tie quarters to a pack. If your elk falls on a steep slope, tying a leg or two to a tree keeps it from sliding. I remember one occasion when I was simply tying my tag to a bull's antler when a slight movement caused him to start sliding. He kept on going for a full 200 yards, which might have been a good thing if my truck was in the bottom of the canyon. But it wasn't. My buddy and I had to pack meat those 200 yards up the mountain. It was not a

QUALITY DAYPACKS, such as this Master Guide Backpack from Crooked Horn Outfitters, are quiet and durable, and keep your hunting accessories dry.

happy time. Rope also may be required to simply hold the elk in position for field-dressing. An elk is so big that it's tough to balance where you can work on it.

Meat bags are somewhat bulky, but are ideal for holding boned meat or quarters, especially if you need to leave the meat and get assistance. The bag can be hung from a tree branch, and the air circulates through it in the breeze. Buy sturdy and reusable meat bags. You can wash them in a washing machine and use them for years. If you don't have room for meat bags, cheesecloth will work, but only temporarily. It's flimsy, it rips and shreds easily, and it allows flies access to the meat through the sparse webbing. Double the amount of cheesecloth you'll need for added strength.

A compact block-and-tackle or lightweight hoist is valuable in lifting meat off the ground where it can be tied to limbs. This item is overlooked by many hunters but comes in extremely handy.

Other accessories depend on the weather, your personal needs and hunting strategies. Some mandatory items include at least one flashlight, preferably two, and a package of fresh batteries. Don't overlook this essential item, even if you're positive you won't be in the woods in the dark. You can never be really sure, because the unexpected can happen. And if you're hunting with a guide, don't trust him to have a flashlight. He may or may not, and if he does the batteries might be weak. I always carry two small flashlights that take AA batteries, and I carry along an eight-pack of fresh batteries. I've learned the hard way that it's no fun making your way through the woods in the dark.

You'll also want a compass and an updated map. If you don't have much experience with a compass and are skeptical, bring two so you can check them against each other. This is really unnecessary, since I've never had a compass that didn't point north, but if it makes you feel better and instills confidence, then do it.

A GPS unit will also help you find your way around. These are remarkable gadgets and have become extremely popular in the last 10 years. The cost has gone down considerably over the years, and a good unit can now be purchased for around $200. Never completely trust a GPS unit if you're headed into unfamiliar country because any electronic device can fail. Always have a compass as a backup if your GPS unit goes haywire.

A small survival kit will likely be unnecessary, but it may save your life if you become lost. The most important item in it are waterproof matches. My favorites are those under the REI brand. They light easily and stay lit in the rain and wind. I keep the

matches and a bit of tinder or firestarter in a sealed Ziploc bag. For tinder I have a small amount of birch bark that I stripped from a dead tree, and a film canister containing six cotton balls soaked with Vaseline. The bark and cotton balls will ignite instantly, and the cotton burns longer.

The kit also holds a small mirror for signaling for help, and a police-type whistle that can be heard far easier than a human shout. A first-aid kit is also included, which holds the usual items such as Band-aids, gauze pads, antiseptic cream, aspirin and medication for nausea, diarrhea and stomachaches.

I also carry a space blanket, a container of water, and trail food that I mix up myself. The latter includes dried bananas, nuts, raisins, dates, sunflower seeds, pumpkin seeds and M&M's.

Orange flagging is useful in marking a route when you leave an animal and return with help to get it out. It's also good to help mark a blood trail, or simply to help you negotiate unfamiliar woods to a spot that you want to return to. Be sure to remove the flagging when it's no longer needed.

An extra jacket or shirt is a good idea if the weather cools, as well as some sort of rain gear. I carry a wool shirt and a lightweight rain jacket and pants that fold into a small package.

Optional gear includes a camera, film, extra food and bugle calls if I'm hunting during the rut. When I'm actually hunting, I carry the call on a string over my shoulder instead of in the pack. I also carry a couple of cow calls in my pocket, regardless of the time of year.

Other accessories include binoculars and a small, lightweight spotting scope if I expect to do any distant glassing, which is almost always. I wear the binoculars on a comfortable neck strap or shoulder harness and stow the scope in my daypack.

A cart with a single wheel is a tremendous asset in getting your meat out of the woods. You can buy a commercial model or make your own. Brakes are a good idea to stop the cart from going downhill faster than you want it to.

Think about the accessories you need and try to include only those that are essential and light. Every ounce adds up, and as you gain experience carrying a pack long distances you'll find ways to minimize the load even more.

Clothing

Mountain country can be unforgiving any time of the year. You can expect snow, hail, rain, wind, heat and cold (perhaps all in one day), and you must be prepared for them. Of course, when you're packing for your trip, you'll have no idea what to expect, so you're apt to throw everything in but the kitchen sink. If you're headed on a backcountry horseback trip, your outfitter might have weight limitations. If you fly, you'll want to pack accordingly, or pay an airline penalty for excess baggage.

A lot of the clothes you choose for your trip will depend on when you hunt elk. September hunts are generally mild, blue-sky days with temperatures in the 70s and higher. But in elk country, September can also bring thunderstorms, heavy rains, days of drizzle and fog, and even snow. For the most part, the bad weather is short-lived, and the weather is balmy. To be on the safe side, bring waterproof apparel and warm clothing. In early October, the aspens are yellow and orange, and frosty mornings are the rule. As fall progresses, you can expect colder nights, with more chances of snow. In November, the mountains are in winter readiness, and you can expect sub-zero temperature and plenty of snow.

CHOOSING HUNTING CLOTHES

When selecting clothing at a store, look for apparel that's made by well-known manufacturers. Invest some money in good clothing; otherwise you might be sorry when you're on the dream trip of your life and you're wet, cold and totally miserable.

The first order of business is to determine if hunter orange is required, and how much and what kind. In some states you must wear a minimum number of

HUNTER ORANGE worn on your head and upper body is the safest way to dress during the firearms season.

square inches, typically 400, which is easily covered by a vest. Orange hats may also be required along with the vest or jacket. In Wyoming, where only one item of orange is required, a hat will suffice. In Colorado, you must wear solid orange, not camo or patterned orange. And so on. If the state you're hunting doesn't require orange, wear it anyway for safety purposes unless you're bowhunting—when orange is never required. Since orange may be your outermost garment for the entire hunt, don't buy a flimsy vest that quickly rips, tears, makes noise and easily gets soaked in wet weather. Buy a quiet and warm waterproof garment. It amazes me that some folks spend a fortune on a hunt, but buy a cheap garment to satisfy the hunter-orange requirement.

Because weather can change quickly in the mountains, the so-called "layered effect" is highly recommended. You might be enjoying a lovely, balmy day,

wearing only a shirt, but when the sun dips below the western horizon you'll likely be reaching for a heavy jacket. When you hike and climb, you'll find yourself taking excess clothes off as you begin to sweat. Perspiration is your worst enemy; avoid it by wearing proper clothing for the occasion. When you perspire, your undergarments get wet; as the weather cools you'll get cold very quickly.

For outer garments, wear clothing made of wool or synthetic materials that are warm, silent and waterproof. Stay away from cotton; in fact, cotton is the worst material to wear in the woods, whether you're wearing it as innerwear or a shirt, sweater or jacket. It quickly soaks through with water and perspiration, and remains cold and clammy for long periods of time. Flannel, by the way, may be either wool or cotton. Down is a superb filling when it's dry, retaining loft and keeping you warm, but when it's wet it's a nightmare. It's almost impossible to dry afield, unless you can hang it on a branch during a hot spell for several hours. If you like down, wear a Gore-tex® or similar waterproof jacket over it. Though it's nice to believe clothing materials that come from nature, such as down and cotton, are the finest, that's not necessarily the case. Many synthetics far outperform natural products.

I have a down jacket that I've been fond of ever since I bought it, but I remember a trip when a downpour turned it into a clammy, heavy, freezing-cold garment. I was mighty unhappy I didn't wear a synthetic waterproof coat that day.

Wool is considered to be the very finest material to wear during adverse weather conditions, but two very memorable hunts come to mind that taught me wool isn't always the answer. One was a hunt in western Washington, when 5 inches of rain fell while we hunted. My wool coat doubled in weight, and it essentially became a giant sponge. I was soaked through and through when I got to camp that night.

The other was an elk hunt in Alberta's Canadian Rockies early in December. One afternoon my companions and I rode horseback up a very high ridge, and when we broke out of the timber into an opening we were hit by a roaring gale that practically knocked our horses off their feet. We dismounted and used our horses as shields as best we could, carefully heading back to the shelter of the trees. I still remember the wind tearing through my heavy wool coat and pants as if I was naked. We learned later that the wind was ripping along at 80 mph, with gusts over 100. The air temperature was down around zero, making the windchill so scary I didn't want to know what it was.

Undergarments are important, since they're the layer that touches the skin. Long johns such as polypropy-

lene or chloropropylene and silk are among the best. They are available for both men and women.

As I mentioned, it's extremely important to keep perspiration to a minimum. Of course, this isn't possible if you're huffing and puffing up a steep slope after an elk, but if you're doing something that's a planned event, like splitting firewood, take some clothes off. Once your undergarments get wet with perspiration, you'll have a tough time warming up if you must remain stationary in the cold, such as while riding a horse back to camp.

A warm hat is extremely important. Though you might have a special relationship with a baseball cap that your youngster gave you for your birthday, it might cause you to half freeze to death on your elk hunt. A baseball cap offers little protection for your ears, and is usually thin enough to allow heat to escape from the top of your head. There's an old saying in the north: "If you want to stay warm, put on a good hat." This is accurate, because much body heat is lost through the head. In extremely cold situations when the wind is blowing hard, wear a balaclava, ski mask or other facial covering.

My wife and I hunted late-season elk in northwest Wyoming in early December one year, and a nasty wind persisted for days, blowing up to 50 mph. The air temperature never got higher than 10°F, and we couldn't expose our faces in the open without some sort of protection. Whenever we left the timber, we put on heavy ski masks, and we never ventured out into the wind for long periods of time.

Gloves are essential in keeping your hands warm, but you'll want the type with a special slit for your trigger finger, or a pair you can quickly remove. Applying trigger pressure is an extremely sensitive task; you must feel the trigger with the skin of your finger, since the shot must be perfectly timed with your hold on the target. For simply walking or sitting, mittens or even a muff will work, but be prepared to quickly extricate your shooting hand.

Consider an appropriate daypack to accommodate the extra clothing you think you'll need on the hunt. If hunting with an outfitter, ask him for a suggested clothing list.

CHOOSING FOOTWEAR

Boots are among the most important apparel item you'll wear. If your feet hurt or get cold, you'll be uncomfortable and likely unwilling to put in a hard day. Do not wear brand-new boots on your hunt. Break them in well before the season, even if you must wear them when mowing the lawn and doing other chores around the house. Before they're broken in, boots are usually stiff and may cause sores and blisters if you suddenly put them through hard use on a hunt.

If the weather is dry and warm, lightweight, waterproof boots are fine. Always think waterproof, no matter how dry you anticipate the weather to be. During cold weather, insulated boots are a must. If you expect to hunt in snow, boots with a leather upper region and rubber on the bottom with felt inserts are a good choice. The felt innershoes can be removed in the evening and dried for the next day's use. They'll typically absorb perspiration from your feet as you walk. I always bring along an extra pair in case the wet ones aren't dry by morning. It's worth repeating: take care of your feet with proper boots. You absolutely won't be able to function if your feet are in pain.

Socks are extremely important, because they're in direct contact with your feet and boots. In very cold weather, I wear a polypropylene sock topped with a heavy wool sock. Before retiring in the evening, I hang the socks to dry if I intend to use them the next day. It's best to change to a clean set daily, but that might not be possible in a backcountry camp where clothing must be minimized.

There are a number of soles available on hunting boots these days. The air-bob type soles are among the best, offering the most traction and grip in slippery country. Air-bobs are round-shaped and about as big as a button. They work amazingly well on snow and slick slopes when most other types of soles fail.

In very cold country, you can use a variety of body warmers by placing them in a pocket, glove or sock. Most of these are packaged so that when you open them, sudden contact with the air causes a chemical reaction, and they heat up. These are welcome if you're sitting quietly for a spell, or if your hands get cold because you've taken your gloves off. In bitterly cold weather, they're welcome any time. Most give off heat an hour or more.

QUALITY RAIN GEAR is an important consideration on any elk hunt. Bowhunters, because they need to get very close to elk in order to take a shot, are wise to invest in camouflaged models made of quiet fabrics, such as Cabela's MT050™ (jacket) and Cabela's Dry-Plus Saddle-Cloth™ (bibs).

Planning an Elk Hunt

Where to Hunt Elk

Once you've decided you want to hunt elk, the first question to ask is, "Where should I go?" Of the 11 western elk states, 10 offer tags to nonresidents. California allows only residents to hunt elk in public drawings, though you can bid on a few tags in auctions. Nevada offers only a dozen or so to nonresidents, as well as providing a couple in auctions, which realistically leaves the remaining nine states to consider for your hunt. There is also a limited elk hunt in Alaska for both resident and nonresident hunters, and many states around the country now offer very limited hunts for residents of those states, though nonresidents may be eligible in some. In most of those states, only a dozen or two elk tags are offered, some each year, and some every other other year. Canada offers outstanding elk hunts to both residents and nonresidents in the provinces of Alberta and British Columbia. Without exception, Americans must hire outfitters in Canada to hunt elk.

Most hunters choose a state based on articles they've read in magazines, conversations they've had with other hunters, outfitter contacts or advertisements, or the ease in getting tags. The latter is often a major consideration, since one of the toughest aspects of planning an elk hunt is getting a tag, especially for nonresidents. With a couple exceptions, residents of elk states can simply purchase a general tag across the counter. Not so for nonresidents, who are commonly faced with the dilemma of obtaining tags in a lottery draw or on a first-come first-served basis.

Of the major elk states, Colorado is the only one offering nonresidents the option of buying a general tag across the counter. Obviously, luck may be a big part of the planning process when other states are being considered, though many now have procedures that assist in drawing tags through a lottery.

UNDERSTANDING ELK TAGS

There are three basic types of tags: general, landowner/outfitter and limited entry. Some states offer one or two options; some offer all three.

The general tag allows the hunter to hunt in any of the units open during a general season, which is usually the same throughout the state, though there are exceptions. Because this season normally has few or no restrictions on hunter numbers, pressure is likely to be heavy on public land having good access.

In states where landowner tags are allowed, the state wildlife agency typically allots a certain number of tags to qualified landowners who then distribute tags as they wish. These tags are usually sold to outfitters who then offer the tags to hunters at a predetermined price. Outfitter tags are offered directly by the wildlife agency to outfitters, who make the tags available to their clients. Landowner tags are usually valid only on a certain property, while outfitter tags are commonly valid on both private and public lands. On Indian reservations, tribes often offer full outfitter services, and sell tags to hunters without state involvement. Most tribal hunts are high quality, with hunter numbers regulated by a quota set by tribal wildlife officers.

Limited-entry tags are authorized only for specific units, and are offered in a lottery draw or by a first-come first-served system, though the former is by far the most common procedure. In a limited-entry unit, biologists set a quota based on the objective of that unit. For example, an overabundance of elk in a unit may require a calculated harvest of cows and calves. In other units, the objective might be to improve the bull/cow ratio or to allow the herd to increase, so a quota of tags is offered. Another objective is to keep hunter numbers low enough to allow a certain number of bulls to escape, live longer and produce larger antlers. This tag is attractive to hunters who prefer a quality hunt offering mature bulls and fewer hunters. In many limited-entry units, public access is good, hunter success is much higher than during general seasons, and trophy bulls are available. Obviously, those tags are highly sought after, and are tough to draw because of competition from other hunters. In some cases, odds of drawing may be 20 to 1 or higher.

To assist hunters in beating the odds of limited-entry units, most states offer some type of system involving either bonus points or preference points. The bonus point is simply an extra application in the drawing. For example, if you have three bonus points, you'll have four applications working for you—the current application, and one each for your three points. One point is allotted each year you apply. Some bonus points are free, and some must be purchased for a modest fee, depending on the state.

The preference-point system allows points to accumulate until the desired number is reached to meet that unit's particular requirement. One preference point is offered each year you apply. Basically, you'll receive your money back if you don't draw the tag, and will receive a preference point. The following year, the procedure is the same, but you'll

receive a second preference point. The next year you'll receive a third preference point. Eventually, if you're persistent, you'll receive enough points to draw the tag. The computer considers only those applications having the highest preference points. For example, assume Unit 1 requires five preference points to draw a tag. You'll need to wait five years, but you're guaranteed a tag. Obviously, the best units have the highest number of preference points required for a tag.

It becomes readily apparent that these systems can be complicated if not downright confusing. Read the applications thoroughly, and be sure you follow instructions explicitly. If you cannot understand them, call the state wildlife agency involved. They have personnel who specifically answer questions from bewildered hunters. On the bright side, the rewards of drawing limited entry tags far outweigh the frustrations of applying.

Other considerations in determining where to hunt involve your objectives. Do you want to see plenty of elk, will you settle for a small bull or cow, or are you after a trophy bull? Remember—all states are not equal. If you had a choice of hunting Florida or Iowa for giant whitetails, for example, you'd choose Iowa. Western states are similar, though big bulls can indeed be found in every state, some more so than others. Arizona, for example, has big bulls, but tags for nonresidents and residents alike must be drawn in a very competitive lottery. I have several friends in that state who have been applying for years but haven't been able to draw a tag.

If you want to see plenty of elk, Colorado may be your best option, but that's entirely up to the circumstances of the hunt. There are far more elk in Colorado than in any other state—in fact, twice the number of the runner-up. But that doesn't mean you'll see twice as many elk as elsewhere, or even any. That's up to you—the hunt area you've chosen, your savvy and your ability to locate elk.

You must give some very serious consideration to the quality of hunting you expect on your trip. If you're looking for solitude, then a wilderness area or a backcountry hunt is in order. Unless you have the means to get back into those remote spots, such as horses and the knowledge to use them, then you're going to need the services of an outfitter. The where-to-go aspect isn't as important here, because the outfitter is counted on to show you elk. It's the do-it-yourself hunt that puts more emphasis on the "where" aspect of your trip.

Hunters who make the decision to hunt general seasons must be well aware of the implications. When I first moved west in 1960 to study forestry, I was dumfounded by the amount of public land where a

person could seemingly hike forever and still never see a posted sign. Coming from the East, it was a breath of fresh air to me. Conversely, I was equally dumfounded when I went on my first hunt and saw so many people I thought I was back East. That's still the case today, so you must resign yourself to that fact of life if you're intending to hunt the general season, especially in a state like Colorado where there are unlimited permits.

Understand that some states have no general licenses, even for residents. Those include Arizona, New Mexico, Nevada and California. In other words, every hunter must apply for each tag in a lottery. An exception in some states is the landowner tag, which you can purchase from the landowner or outfitter who leases his land. You are entitled to hunt that particular piece of property, though there might be some exceptions.

In Wyoming, where I live, general licenses are purchased over the counter by residents, but nonresidents must apply for them in a lottery. Once you've drawn the tag, you are then entitled to hunt every unit in the state that is open to general hunting, and, of course, you must abide by the specific season allowed in each unit. You may not hunt in a limited-entry, or draw area, with a general tag. This system is essentially the same in other western states.

Many hunters decide where they want to hunt by the ease of getting a tag. A common strategy is to apply for a limited-entry tag in a state like Idaho, Wyoming or Montana, or even a general tag—if the tag isn't drawn, then the hunter goes to Colorado, where nonresident tags can be purchased over the counter.

Once again, and I repeat because this is an exceedingly important point: If crowded woods bother you, then don't hunt during general seasons where pressure is high. Be aware, too, that in states with fewer hunters, such as Wyoming, there are far fewer hunters in general units than there would be in neighboring Colorado. The bottom line is always the same: the quality of elk hunting always increases as the number of hunters decreases.

If it seems like I'm treating Colorado unfairly in terms of too many hunters and poor-quality hunting, that's only partially correct. Truth is, this state offers superb hunting in limited-entry areas, as do all states in their limited-entry areas.

As this book is written, I now have 11 preference points for Colorado. In other words, I've been applying each year since I hunted a limited-entry unit 12 years ago. That hunt, incidentally, was superb. In that unit, I hunted public land with good road access, saw plenty of bulls and few hunters, and ended up

QUALITY ELK HABITAT is easy to find throughout much of the West. The "catch" is that you can't simply buy a license over the counter to hunt these places. Instead, you must apply for limited-entry tags in several states on a yearly basis. If you consistently apply for these tags, you'll eventually draw a tag to hunt in a high-quality area.

taking a nice six-point bull 300 yards from my pick-up. This is the norm on top-quality limited-entry hunts. I should point out that one need not wait a dozen years to draw a tag. Each unit has its own number of point requirements, depending on the popularity and quality of the area. Many units require only three or four points for a tag.

Curiously, comparatively few hunters, even Colorado residents, apply for these limited-entry tags. Each year at my elk-hunting seminars I ask my audience how many of them are applying for tags. Typically, less than 10 percent of them try. Puzzled, I sought to find out why. Here are some of the reasons: 1) Hunters complain that applications are too complicated, and don't take the time to figure them out. 2) Hunters claim they're unlucky and never draw anything in a lottery. (This has nothing to do with it. Preference points accumulate—once you have enough, you draw a tag. Period.) 3) Hunters are too impatient and don't want to wait several years to draw. (In truth, many units have a short wait. Besides, even if you don't draw you get your money back, and you can still hunt the general season that fall.) 4) Hunters

don't want to hunt a new area, preferring to camp with their pals in their traditional spot. (That's fine and understandable, but why not try a special place where the odds are in your favor—where you can finally put that dream bull on the wall?) 5) Hunters are unaware of limited-entry units. (I find this reason virtually impossible. These units are well known and talked about in hunter circles every day).

I'm using Colorado as an example. As I explained earlier in this chapter, many states have preference and bonus points to help draw those coveted tags. When you're making a decision as to where to hunt, why not start applying for points in two or three states? At some point you'll surely draw a tag.

Remember, too, that when you decide on where to go, you must consider your physical limitations and the availability of gear to move an elk in the woods. The latter is a big deal; don't take it lightly. You must also consider the terrain, remoteness of the area and a host of other factors. Planning an elk hunt requires plenty of homework. Do it well and you'll likely experience the hunting trip of a lifetime.

Choosing an Outfitter

The decision to hire an outfitter depends on the status of your bank account, your personal preference and the type of hunt you're going on. Outfitters provide several services, including land access, transportation to and from the hunting area, guides, food, accommodations and hauling your elk out of the woods.

OUTFITTER PROS AND CONS

Should you hire an outfitter? There are advantages and disadvantages, with sound arguments on each side. Perhaps the most important advantage is less competition from other hunters. When you come right down to it, low elk-hunting pressure translates to quality hunting and a far better chance of being successful.

Land access is an extremely important plus, whether you're riding horseback into the backcountry or hunting private land leased by the outfitter. If your heart is set on a trek to the hinterlands, your only option is horse or mule, unless you're an NFL tackle who can carry an oversized backpack for several miles. Since most of us don't have the luxury of owning stock animals, an outfitter makes great sense.

Of course, outfitters aren't particularly fond of hauling hunters and gear a dozen miles or more into the wilderness, given the logistical problems, liability and plain tough work. They do it because wilderness areas offer the best elk hunting. Your odds of taking a nice bull are considerably higher in the backcountry, and the tranquility and challenge of a mountain hunt are icing on the cake.

I don't know how many wilderness hunts I've been on, but every one was special, whether it was in Idaho's Selway, Montana's Anaconda-Pintler, Wyoming's Washakie or Colorado's Neversummer. All have one thing in common—a feeling of remoteness and tranquility. These enormous tracts of backcountry were designated by the U.S. Congress, and are destined to remain forever wild. No logging, mining, or other uses are permitted, nor are any kinds of gasoline engines. For the backcountry hunter, that means wood must be cut by hand, and no generators will light up tents. Wheels of any kind are also strictly prohibited.

If you want to warm up in a hurry, try cutting a big batch of firewood with a crosscut saw and splitting it with an axe. When you want light at night, don't look to a light bulb, but fire up a lantern. And if you must haul something heavy, don't look for a wheelbarrow or a cart; carry it in your arms, on your back, or on your horse. These are just some of the unique hardships you'll endure on a wilderness hunt, notwithstanding the fact that help and civilization are usually a long hike or horseback ride away.

You can rent horses and make the trip on your own, but you'd better be well-versed in horsemanship. You'll need the savvy to tie knots properly and pack correctly, and the wisdom to solve problems on the trail. Few hunters have those talents, thus the need for an outfitter's services.

An outfitter also offers knowledge, a necessary ingredient for any form of hunting. He should be familiar with the trail network in his territory and aware of elk movement patterns and feeding and bedding areas.

Having said that, I can also state from firsthand experience that some outfitters are ripoff artists who will sell you not a dream trip but a nightmare. I remember an elk hunt with a person claiming to be an outfitter that was perhaps the biggest joke I'd seen in a lifetime of hunting. I didn't arrange this hunt, but went along as a guest of a businessman who had never been elk hunting before. The businessman relied on one of his salesmen to set up the hunt.

It was supposed to be a backcountry affair with horses, guides and all the accouterments of an outfitted hunt. There were five of us in all, anticipating an enjoyable elk hunt in beautiful surroundings.

I drove to the hunt in my pickup; the others traveled by plane. We met at the airport, and the outfitter was an hour late. No big deal, but he had a feeble

excuse and didn't seem to be telling the truth. It got worse from there.

Instead of a backcountry camp, we discovered that camp was set directly under a huge utility line with a half dozen wires sizzling and humming overhead. The spot was less than 1 mile from a paved road, next to a very large river. There was no outhouse; we were told to "find us a spot in the woods." Not only were there no horses, but there was no corral or any means to tie horses up, and I noted there wasn't much grass either. The only positive thing about the whole scenario was the condition of the tents. They were brand new, which told me something about the outfitter.

Toward dusk a pickup towing a large horse trailer showed up. A man wearing a battered hat and a big smile got out and asked if the outfitter was around. The man said he was hired on

EXPERIENCED GUIDES know when to move on a bull and when to stay put. Their split-second decisions often result in the client taking home a quality bull (inset).

as the wrangler and guide, and confided to me later that he'd never been in that country before. As we later learned, the outfitter hadn't been in that country before, and he was terrified of horses. He also knew next to nothing about elk hunting.

This hunt was a disaster, and we found out that the outfitter saw a way to make an easy dollar and posed himself as an expert. It was a shame, because the man who paid for the hunt was swindled by a clever crook.

That was an extreme case, but hundreds of other hunters are bilked each year by dishonest people portraying themselves as outfitters.

No outfitted hunt can be guaranteed to produce an elk. There are too many variables influencing your trip, such as weather, elk behavior and your ability

to meet the challenges of the hunt. Many people believe an outfitted hunt is relatively easy because of the availability of horses and guides, and the fact you're in prime country. But be aware you might have to hike up and down steep terrain and have the endurance to perform according to your guide's instructions. Most guides are in far better physical condition than their clients, and the typical high altitudes in elk country make comparatively easy chores more difficult. Count on sore muscles, excessive fatigue and a fond yearning for a sleeping bag after each day's hunt.

DEALING WITH ELK GUIDES

Some guides have an attitude problem with respect to their clients. Guides feel the hunter should be able to maintain a guide's pace, forgetting that the hunter is perhaps in poor physical condition. Young guides have little understanding of aches and pains associated with middle age and beyond, and can't comprehend why a person can't keep up. This isn't necessarily the fault of the guide, simply blissful ignorance.

Guides are usually proud, young people who are competitive, which is a common human trait. They want their clients to score so they'll have credibility in camp. Some guides may wager on whose client takes the biggest bull, or the quickest bull. That being the case, they might urge you up the mountain a little faster to get to the top when the bull is there, or push you along a sparse path in the timber faster than you care to go. It's natural for them to move fast; it may be dangerous for you to do so if you aren't in shape. If you feel like you're exerting yourself beyond safe levels, it's time to sit down and have a chat with your guide. Politely tell him that he'll keep your pace, and you don't intend to keep his, reminding him that you're paying for the hunt and you want to return home alive and well. This is no time to be stubborn and try to perform as he does, because you could easily hurt yourself.

It would be wonderful if all guides were competent and savvy to elk and elk behavior, but that's not the case. These people don't get paid high wages, and their work is seasonal. Many take higher-paying jobs, and the outfitter must continually search for replacements. Unfortunately, many have no business being guides at all.

I've been in situations where the guide had spent only a day or two in the country he was guiding in, and I've seen guides who didn't carry binoculars, flashlights or sharp knives. Many guides don't have the ability to judge an elk's antlers, often getting too excited and insisting the client shoot a bull that's smaller than the client desired.

Having said this, I'll say I've met many top-notch elk-hunting guides. If you have a problem with your guide, speak to the outfitter about the situation. Personalities may clash, and the last thing you want on your hunt is a problem you don't need. To complicate the situation, some hunters are so full of themselves and so egotistical they don't trust any guide. The worst hunters are those who know a little about elk hunting, and think they know it all. One can't blame some guides and outfitters for being hard on a hunter if he has an unpleasant personality.

Of all the things you'll appreciate on an outfitted hunt, you'll be most happy with the comparative ease in getting your elk out of the mountains. In the backcountry, your outfitter does this by quartering or boning the animal and transporting it on horses. In camps more accessible to vehicles, he may be able to drive to it with a pickup or ATV. In either case, the need to move several hundred pounds of meat over awful terrain is a serious task that must be dealt with without hurting yourself. You can indeed hurt yourself if you don't have the means to move an elk's carcass.

Another advantage to hiring an outfitter is having your basic daily living needs, as in eating and sleeping, tended to. Your meals are provided, and you'll have a bed, though it might be a simple cot in a tent heated by a woodstove. In some cases, you might be quartered in a cabin, a ranch house, or an elegant lodge, depending on the outfitter's accommodations.

Don't be fooled into thinking that just because you're in a tent with a woodstove you'll be comfy all night. If you're hunting when the nights get cold, which is almost always in elk country, rest assured that the fire in the stove will go out about 2 hours after you've gone to bed. If your sleeping bag is meant for cool summer nights, you'll soon be aware of a serious drop in air temperature inside the tent. The only solution at the time is to throw a couple of chunks of wood in the stove, and keep up that routine every hour or two. However, when your guide tells you it's wake-up time at 4 A.M., you'll be miserable and tired. A better solution is to bring your best cold-weather sleeping bag. If you don't have one, buy or borrow one. Sleep is an important commodity on an elk hunt. Get as much as you can.

The best sleeping bag made won't keep you warm if you sleep on a cot; the cold air under the cot chills you to the bone. To resolve this dilemma, simply sleep on the ground with a foam pad, either open or closed cell. If you don't have a pad and must sleep on a cot, spread soft garments on the cot to provide temporary insulation.

There are a couple of disadvantages to an outfitted hunt, the major one being cost. You can expect to pay several thousand dollars for a hunt; in the case of some ranches and Indian reservations, the figure may be in the five-digit range. Another disadvantage is the need to comply with the rules of camp. You'll be eating, sleeping and hunting according to the wishes of a stranger who may not schedule your day according to the manner in which you're accustomed. Small discomforts may become apparent, and you won't have much flexibility in changing them. That's a necessary aspect of hunting with an outfitter, and the reason you tolerate it is, of course, the opportunity of getting within range of a big bull elk.

Unfortunately, that dream bull might be only a fantasy if you've hooked up with an outfitter who doesn't fulfill his end of the deal. As I mentioned, there are no guaranteed hunts; the sad fact is that many outfitters are crooks, pure and simple.

BOOKING AN OUTFITTER

So how do you select an outfitter who is honest and capable of meeting your expectations—one that won't fleece you as in the account I related earlier? You can contact outfitters in several ways: through magazine advertisements, at sportsmen's shows and conventions, TV ads, direct mail, referrals from acquaintances, or through a booking agent.

The latter is the most reliable, because agents carefully screen their stable of outfitters, working only with those who meet high standards. Unfortunately, some agents work on the shady side—in their eagerness to make a commission they deal with questionable outfitters. To be on the safe side, work with agents who have been in business for at least 15 years. You pay no more to book with an agent, since the commission is paid by the outfitter and not the client. For example, a $3,500 elk hunt costs that much whether you book it through an agent or directly from the outfitter.

Good agents personally visit every camp they represent. Reputable people like Gregg Severinson of Cabela's Outdoor Adventures and the Atchesons of Jack Atcheson and Sons are skilled hunters and among the best hunters I know. When they book you with an outfitter, they've checked him out thoroughly and approve of his operation.

That doesn't mean, however, the outfitter they recommend is infallible and will meet your highest expectations. Being human, outfitters have weaknesses. Like you, they have a personal life. They may divorce, get sick, have mental problems, start abusing alcohol, go nearly bankrupt, lose their best guides and suffer all sorts of minor disasters. You can only hope that everything runs smooth when you hunt, but there are never any guarantees.

Meeting outfitters in person at shows and conventions isn't necessarily a safe option. Many shysters talk a good line, and will have you convinced their operation is the best in the West.

I recall an outfitter at a sportsmen's show who talked a great line. He was easy to spot, wearing a pretty monogrammed shirt, with buttons opened down to his chest, a gold necklace wrapped around his neck, and shiny teeth surrounded by a wide smile. This guy could talk the talk, and he booked hunters with amazing ease. But he was a crook. He was finally convicted of racketeering and spent time in jail.

On the other hand, I know outfitters who are shy and quiet, sitting back in their booths and hardly being social. They don't talk much, and hate being in the big city. Prospective clients usually pass them by, considering them country bumpkins who couldn't possibly offer a good elk hunt. Truth be known, those are the real woodsmen, the kind of people who can put you on a quality elk hunt.

Before booking a trip, be sure you are clearly aware of every detail, from the quality and quantity of elk in the hunt area, to the hunting techniques, to the rigors of the hunt itself. The outfitter will undoubtedly give you a list of references. Call instead of writing, and ask the people you talk to for names of other hunters in their camp. Every outfitter will list only the happy hunters; you should talk to everyone for a clear picture of the hunt.

If you're riding to camp on a horse, find out if there are weight limitations, and pack your gear wisely. Always use duffel bags, never hard-sided suitcases, because the latter are tougher to pack and balance on a horse. If the horseback trip is long, get off the horse and lead it downhill every now and then to give you a chance to use weary muscles. By walking briskly on a good trail, you should be able to keep up the pace of the rest of the party. Always tie a waterproof jacket behind the saddle, even if the day promises to be bright and balmy. Weather can change quickly in the mountains.

I recall many trips when hunters didn't heed the advice of outfitters and either didn't tie a quality raincoat behind the saddle at all or tied on a cheap one. When the weather turned bad they were sorry, drenched and much wiser. On one trip, the sky opened in a drenching downpour. We were caught on a high mountain pass, and everyone but one hunter had appropriate clothing. His raingear was tucked away in a duffel bag firmly packed on a horse. The outfitter could have looked the other way and kept going, but he was a considerate guy and tied up the entire string along the trail. He untied the pack, found the correct bag, opened it up and retrieved the rain gear. About that time one of the mules balked at the load it was carrying and began crowhopping and carrying on. He unnerved a couple of other mules and horses, and presently we had a little rodeo on the ridge. When the stomping and kicking was over, the outfitter had to pick up gear and duffels scattered all over the slope, repack and retie everything, and generally put everything back in working order. He and his guides did it without mumbling much, and we made it to camp an hour later than we expected.

Your decision to hire an outfitter depends on your personal requirements. You must determine your physical ability to make a backcountry hunt if that's the nature of the trip, and, of course, you must decide if you can afford it. Don't be surprised to learn that a successful outfitted hunt, in the long run, may be cheaper than a series of failed do-it-yourself hunts.

Do-It-Yourself Elk Hunts

Every year, thousands of elk are taken by hunters who do it on their own. Given the enormity of elk country and the task of getting a very large animal out of the woods, this is a formidable task.

The nature of land ownership in the West allows plenty of hunting opportunities. Tens of millions of acres of U.S. Forest Service and Bureau of Land Management lands (the former an agency within the Department of Agriculture, the latter the Department of Interior) offer public hunting in every elk state.

When I first journeyed west in 1960 to study forestry at Utah State University, I was absolutely amazed at the lack of posted signs. It boggled my mind to think that I could walk and hike for weeks on public land and never have to ask for permission. Having lived in the West for more than 35 years, I'm still amazed, and appreciative, that those public lands are still there.

Some of these lands can be accessed directly from major highways, or they may be wilderness areas deep in the backcountry. And there's thousands of miles of dirt roads in every state that take you into or near prime elk country. Camping is widely available, either in designated campgrounds or randomly at convenient locations, depending on the rules of the administering land agency. Modest fees may be charged in campgrounds, though many are officially closed after tourist season ends and are available at no charge to hunters. Check at the campground entrances for details. If campgrounds are closed, water systems will be shut down and you'll need a supply of water. Outhouses may or may or may not be locked, depending on the circumstances, so you'll need to check into this necessary matter.

When you've made the decision to hunt on your own, immediately send for state hunting regulations. Write or call the wildlife agency, or look it up on the Internet. All states now have websites, and you'll find most, if not all, the information you'll need.

Carefully fill out your application, if one is required, and be sure to mail it with applicable funds long before the deadline. If you're applying in a lottery, familiarize yourself with preference and bonus-point options that increase your odds in drawing a tag.

When you know the tags are forthcoming, send away for maps of the area you'll be hunting. Both the Forest Service and BLM sell maps for a modest fee, generally less than $5. Look for campsite possibilities, and acquaint yourself with the road system. Check for spots as far off the beaten track as you can, though this might not be possible during general season where hunter pressure is high.

HORSES are a great asset to the do-it-yourself hunter. Not only do horses help hunters pack in equipment, they help pack out elk meat.

When doing your homework for the hunt, call wildlife officers and inquire as to areas you might hunt. While this might seem to be an imposition, most wildlife workers willingly offer valuable information. I worked as a wildlife biologist for the federal government, and was always pleased to talk to hunters.

You should ask general questions, never specific ones. For example, you might ask for some locations where a hunter might find some decent elk hunting.

Keeping the Trust

When someone goes out of his way to show you a favorite hunting spot, ethics require you to keep that information to yourself. If you return with your brother-in-law's cousin or your boss's nephew, who then return with their friends at a later date, you can count on losing your original source as a friend. If you return, go back with a trusted companion or two and ask your local pal if it's okay before you plan the trip, even if you're hunting public land. Insure him that your buddies have promised to keep the area privy only to your group and no one else.

If, on the other hand, you ask the spot where the person hunts, then you're treading on thin ice. No one wants to divulge special hunting spots, and you might irritate the person and find the rest of the dialogue unproductive. Try to keep your conversation short, and ask the person if you can call back should you need more information.

Ideally, make a summer visit to your hunting spot and spend as much time as you can looking over the area. Most people can't afford to take two vacations a year, but a preliminary scouting session is highly recommended. You might take your family along on a general vacation and squeeze in a day or two investigating the area you'll be hunting later in the fall. In the chapter of this book titled, "Scouting," (p.74) I give specific details on how and where to scout for elk.

The best way to hunt an unfamiliar area without an outfitter is to go with some acquaintances who know the country and can give you some rough ideas of where to hunt. Be wary of the guy in the saloon who offers to semi-guide you for cash under the table. Not only is this illegal in most states, but you'll likely be taken for a ride and never see an elk.

he was kind enough to share information with me as to places to hunt. He put X's on maps, gave me some insights on avoiding other hunters, and pointed out elk feeding and bedding areas he'd located.

Many bed-and-breakfasts are springing up around the country. Many B&B's not only accommodate hunters for a week or more, but also provide lunches and dinners. An obvious advantage here is the fact that you'll be sharing a home with residents who, like the motel owner I mentioned above, may have information about local hunting.

I stayed at a B&B once, but I wasn't elk hunting, and had no plans to hunt because I didn't know the area—in fact, I hunted another place about 100 miles away. As it turned out, the owner's daughter was married to a man who was an avid elk hunter. I met him after breakfast, and we talked about elk and elk hunting the rest of the morning. He had the day off from work, took me for a ride in the forest, and subsequently invited me to return in the future to hunt with him and his family. I did, and enjoyed plenty of camaraderie as well as excellent hunting.

It's important to remember that our modern society seems to have caused us to wall ourselves off from one another. Distrust of fellow humans is an unfortunate attitude these days, but I've found that people are quick to open up and hit it off if you make a good impression. Hunting engenders even more distrust because it's so competitive. I've found that a friendly attitude and a quick smile opens many doors that normally are closed.

If you intend to camp in a public campground, you might face plenty of crowding from other hunters. Try to arrive at least 2 days before the season opens. This is also true if you intend to camp along a road, since the choice spots are taken first. Your options are tents, cabover pickup campers, travel trailers or motor homes.

If you decide to camp in a tent, choose a roomy model with plenty of space to accommodate your beds and gear. A wall tent with a woodstove is the best option, since they offer plenty of room, head space and the means to dry wet clothing. The latter is extremely important but often overlooked. If you can't get dry you'll be miserable, wet and cold, and you won't be enthusiastic about hunting.

My favorite tent is the standard wall tent outfitted with a woodstove; a portable table with a two-burner stove; a lightweight cabinet stocked with pots, pans and sundries; cots; and portable stools. I set the tent up away from dead trees or leaners, which could come down in a windstorm, and away from tall trees, which might invite a lightning strike. I cover the roof with a large tarp that is lashed securely to aid in

TYPES OF HUNTS

There are five basic ways you can hunt on your own: 1) base out of a motel; 2) stay in campgrounds or along a road on public land (where allowed); 3) base out of a ranchhouse or cabin on private land; 4) backpack into the mountains; or 5) use an outfitter's drop camp.

Using a motel as a base isn't as illogical as it sounds, especially if you're hunting a limited-entry area that isn't crowded with other hunters. In any case, plenty of elk can be found within hiking distance of major roads. The downside is you might have to arise several hours earlier in the morning to drive to where you'll be hunting. The advantage is you'll be in a warm, comfy room with hot showers and cafes close by. If you opt to stay in a motel, be aware they're commonly booked well in advance of elk season, especially in small towns close to elk country. A call to the local Chamber of Commerce is advised to help plan your stay.

For years I hunted one spot and stayed in a small motel close to the unit because elk could be found fairly close to roads and there were no campgrounds in the vicinity. The motel operator was a hunter, and

Wall tent with woodstove and portable table

keeping out a heavy rain. Many tents, no matter how well made, have the nasty habit of leaking during a downpour or under a load of snow. When erecting the tent, I position it so the door faces away from the prevailing wind direction. If possible, I'll bring firewood from home, but I'm more likely to cut it near the site. Always check with the public agency involved since you might need to buy a firewood permit and cut only in designated areas. I should mention that although a tent offers a real sense of hunting and being in the outdoors, I quite often use a travel trailer because it's easy to set up when I'm in a hurry, which seems to be a fact of life with me. The tent is a luxury when I have time, and is sometimes mandatory if I'm camping along a rugged secondary road that is inaccessible with my camp trailer.

Cabover pickup campers are popular, but you should have the option of dropping off the unit beside the road and using the truck for travel. Most units can be quickly off-loaded. What you don't want is the burden of turtle-backing your camper to your hunting unit, since low tree branches may block your route. Then too, every time you want to drive you must carefully store everything in the unit so things don't roll around and fall to the floor as you're moving.

My first camp unit (other than a tent) was a cabover snugged into the bed of my pickup. It was an unwieldy thing, requiring plenty of effort to load and unload, and had tight quarters. Two adults were about all that could be comfortably accommodated. Nonetheless I used it for years, and made it much easier on myself by installing jacks that raised and lowered the unit on and off the bed, not only for off-season storage, but also when I hunted. That way, I could leave the camper at the site for the duration of the hunt and have my truck free to use without the cumbersome load.

Since the camper takes up all the space in your pickup bed, bring along a large tarp you can lay on the floor for transporting elk meat home. The tarp keeps both the floor and the meat clean.

Travel trailers are easily towed and unhitched. Depending on the size, they generally offer more room than cabover units. The downside is the need to tow them over rugged roads and to maneuver in tight spaces. The trailer also precludes the possibility of towing a second hunting vehicle.

My standard camp rig is a 17½-foot camp trailer that meets all my needs. It's large enough to accommodate three adults, and short enough to squeeze into areas with limited space. If I'm hunting late in the fall, I'll empty the water tanks and pipes and winterize the unit. I bring at least 15 gallons of water in three large containers. I also make sure the battery is fully charged, and I bring a spare battery just in case. The propane tanks are filled, and I make sure the stove, lights (both interior and exterior) and furnace are in working order before I leave home.

If you aren't adept at towing trailers, have a companion direct you as you back up, especially if you're trying to position the unit among some trees. Be aware of uneven ground as well. A stout sagebrush bush may tear out a pipe or punch a hole in one of the holding tanks. I've experienced both those problems, and I've also had tree branches make some serious scratches along the side walls.

Motor homes are not recommended in elk country unless you intend to park the unit very close to an all-weather road and are towing a hunting vehicle, which is fairly common. Motor homes are next to useless on snowy, icy roads. I can recall many occasions where people drove motor homes deep into the forest when the roads were dry, only to have them miserably stuck after a sudden winter storm. During one trip, a furious blizzard piled 2 feet of snow overnight in the high country. At least 50 hunting parties were camped along a huge ridge, and everyone tried to get out at the same time. A motor home was solidly stuck in a snow drift, and it took a tow truck from a nearby town to get it free. As you can imagine, more than 100 elk hunters were not thinking fond thoughts about the driver of that motor home. I waited nearly 6 hours to get out.

Make sure your camp unit is completely winterized if you're hunting elk any time after early October. Freezing weather and even subzero temperatures are possible in the high country, and your waterlines will freeze—you can take that to the bank.

Do not bring a two-wheel drive vehicle on an elk hunt. You'll need a four-wheel drive to negotiate many forest roads, especially if it's stormy. Many mountain roads become almost impassible with mud when it rains or the snow melts. Chains, a sturdy jack, a shovel, a tow strap, jumper cables and tools are necessary. Remember that your cell phone might not be within range of a tower; you're apt to be incommunicado.

I've been involved in so many incidents where our vehicles were stuck that I can't remember them all. Having driven a four-wheel drive pickup truck all my adult life, I can say from experience that a four-wheel drive also gets you stuck farther back in the woods than a two-wheel drive. And just because you have a winch and a jack doesn't mean you're home free. I was hunting with a buddy in western Washington when he buried the truck to the axles in thick mud. My pal boasted that we'd be out in a jiffy, and began fiddling with a winch mounted on the front bumper. Unfortunately the winch did not work. The next step was to jack the truck up and put some branches and rocks under each tire, but the jack didn't work either. We had worked with shovels for several hours, making little progress, when another bunch of hunters came by. They had a working winch on their truck, and saved the day by pulling us out of the miserable mud hole.

Before you go on your elk hunt, take your vehicle to a mechanic. Have it tuned and lubed, and have all parts checked for wear, especially belts. Always remember Murphy, whose law may come back to haunt you if you aren't prepared.

PRIVATE VS. PUBLIC LAND

If you're hunting private land, you might have accommodations on the ranch property. Be sure to find out in advance what supplies you'll need, such as sleeping bags, towels, lanterns, generators, cooking utensils, etc. Some outbuildings and cabins have no electricity or water.

If you've had any experience in the West, you'll soon learn the best hunting is often on private lands. This isn't always the case, but it's true enough of the time that you'll be frustrated because those lands are almost always posted. This is due to the pattern in which the West was settled.

When the pioneers arrived, they staked their homesites on fertile, accessible ground, with adequate water nearby. As a result, most valleys and lowlands were quickly gobbled up by a tough breed of humans who fought many hardships, including droughts, insect plagues, floods, hostile Indians and others in order to survive. The government allowed them to settle tracts of lands in blocks of 40 acres, most commonly 160-acre tracts. As the years passed,

FOUR-WHEEL DRIVE VEHICLES (above) are a must for the do-it-yourself elk hunter. The weather can change quickly in mountainous country, and without a four-wheel drive you'll often be left waiting for help instead of looking for elk.

many of those lands were traded or sold to neighbors, and families pooled their properties to establish large blocks of ownership.

In the early 1900s, the Forest Service was established, and the federal government took over management of much of the unsettled and unclaimed timbered lands, which were subsequently divided up into the national forests we know today. About 192 million acres are currently in the U.S. Forest Service system. There were other lands, most of them in lower elevations that didn't have forest resources but included deserts, prairies, rimrock country and landscapes no one else wanted. These eventually were administered by the U.S. Bureau of Land Management, a comparatively new agency of the Department of the Interior. Those lands, known as BLM lands, amount to about 270 million acres, most of them in the West and Alaska.

A good share of those public lands are leased by private individuals who graze livestock on them, but the leases are only for grazing, and access cannot be denied to the public. In some situations, usually on BLM lands, ranchers have been known to illegally post public land. This isn't a major problem, but it happens occasionally. If you encounter this situation, and are positive you're correct, call the sheriff's office, report the violation and alert the government agency administering the land.

Because of the patchwork of land ownership, some prime elk country on public land is literally blocked

BACKPACK CAMPS offer elk hunters the ultimate in solitude. With proper planning, backpacking is a great way to escape the heavy hunting pressure often found near roads.

because it's surrounded on one or more sides by posted private land. Many government tracts are completely surrounded by private properties. What this means is hunters do not have access to those public lands; this has been a great source of controversy for as long as I can remember.

However, an enterprising hunter with a good updated map and the willingness to do some research can often find routes to partially blocked public lands. You can do this by purchasing either a BLM or Forest Service map of the area you want to hunt, and checking out the ownership patterns. Both these government maps clearly show boundaries. I've found that by carefully drawing those boundaries on a topographic map, which doesn't show property ownerships but includes many more details than government maps, you'll have a reliable guide that allows you to access public land without trespassing. I use colored pencils to highlight the area I'm interested in hunting. Remember, private property isn't often fenced in the West, and in many states the landowner doesn't have to post the land. It's incumbent on the hunter to know precisely where he or she is hunting. In some states, however, private lands must be posted with either a sign or a dab of orange paint, and the markers must be placed at distances stipulated by state law.

If you decide to try hiking to those public lands by taking a route around private property, be aware that you might have a big chore ahead of you. You might have to walk several miles over extremely rugged terrain, and you must always anticipate some means of getting an elk out if you score.

One way to eliminate a daily grueling hike in and out is to backpack and take your camp with you. I've

done it a number of times, and have plenty of memories—most of them good. An option for getting your elk out is to make arrangements with a packer prior to going in, and pay him to transport your elk on his horses.

Backpack camping is only for the sound of mind and body. Not only are you carrying all your gear on your back, but you need to transport your elk out as well. This could be the ordeal of the decade if you aren't conditioned and don't have the appropriate gear. Use a sturdy, reliable, lightweight pack frame, and include a lightweight, waterproof tent, sleeping bag, foam pad, and only the essential items you'll need. Plan your meals carefully and consider your water needs.

Pay particular attention to your choice of tents. Once I bought a new state-of-the-art tent that was almost guaranteed to keep you alive atop Mount Everest. Unfortunately, I didn't check it out or prep it before I used it. A steady rain caused several leaks, and my nice waterproof tent wasn't living up to its reputation. I later learned I needed to seal each seam with a sealer that came in a tube along with the tent. I didn't read the directions thoroughly, other than to figure out how to set up the tent. Had I done so, I'd have spent a dry night in the woods.

Backpack hunting is a superb option if you're hunting an area where hunter pressure is heavy. You can camp away from roads and let hunters push elk to you early in the morning, when most other people are beginning to leave roads and trails.

Drop camps are ideal if you don't want to spend the time to scout unfamiliar country. An outfitter typically packs your party to a camp he's set up ahead of time, and leaves you to hunt on your own. He'll return when the hunt is over and pack you and your game back out. He might check on you every other day or so to pack meat or see what supplies you might need. Don't depend on the camp having all the necessary items you'll need. For example, bring in extra lantern mantles, an axe, and other camp items that have a way of breaking or otherwise becoming useless. Find out precisely what the outfitter provides, and determine if you must transport your elk to camp or if he'll pick it up at the site of the kill. This is an extremely important bit of information to know and agree upon.

At first glance, a drop camp seems like the best of all worlds. After all, you'll be packed into elk country and have the ability to hunt on your own, with all your gear and transportation needs taken care of—and all for a reasonable price. But drop camps have a reputation of being iffy, since some unscrupulous outfitters set camps in marginal country where there are few or no elk. They do this because it's easier to pack a camp and hunters a short distance from the trailhead, and also because they might want to keep drop-camp hunters from competing with their fully-guided and higher-paying customers who are hunting prime country. In some cases, outfitters are operating in poor elk country but nonetheless set up drop camps anyway. An outfitter probably won't tell you exactly where the drop camp location is, but if you can learn its general location you can contact the wildlife agency and learn about elk populations thereabouts, the quality of bulls and other information. Many hunters take pride in doing hunts on their own, and there's a special satisfaction by doing so. But do your planning well before the trip. There's no such thing as too much planning.

How NOT to Get Lost

One of the biggest fears among many hunters is getting lost. Because of the vast country in the West, along with heavy timber and mountains stretching away as far as the eye can see, it's a very real problem, especially if the weather is bad.

Unless you've been lost, and I mean hopelessly lost where you have no idea where you are and how to get out of the woods, you can't begin to understand the hysteria and panic that overcomes you.

I was lost once, when I was 18 years old. Three of us were hunting whitetails in northern New York State, in a swamp stretching into Canada for dozens of miles. My two pals and I had taken a small motorboat into the swamp, and merely struck out into the forest with no compasses or maps. We were students at a forestry college, and considered ourselves infallible in the woods. At that age, we figured we could do no wrong.

The weather turned nasty as a snowstorm rolled in, bringing with it a drop in the temperature. We continued to hunt, and when it was time to leave we each struck off in a different direction. Each of us believed we were right, and soon we realized our predicament. The next couple of hours were chaotic, and I was sure we were going to die in the swamp, just as some other hunters had done years before.

Suddenly we heard shots nearby, and found a couple of hunters who had shot at a black bear that we'd pushed toward them. They told us how to get to our boat, and we found it before dark. The experience is one I'll never forget, and I can still feel the fear.

I've been turned around a number of times since then, but I've always kept my wits about me and found my way out. A compass is with me at all times, and I've never left home without one if I was headed into rugged or remote country.

It's amazing how many hunters don't carry a compass, and if they do, are unaware of how to use it. I carry two, just in case one breaks, and to insure that they both point north. They always do, of course, and I know better because I spent a good share of my life working as a forest ranger, but I always like the reinforcement of a second compass, just in case.

Of course, a shining sun tells you direction all day long, but it can't be counted on to shine. When it clouds up, there's no way to tell. Incidentally, moss doesn't always grow on the north side of trees, and other directional myths are just that—myths.

To learn how to use a compass, buy one of the many books on the subject. It shouldn't take you more than an hour to learn the basics of bearings, magnetic declinations and other associated terms. You also need to learn to read a map, which is simple. Understanding contour lines, distance scales and map symbols are the essential points. A compass and updated map are the only tools you need to find your way around in the woods.

When I hunt, I like to determine a base line that I can refer to when it's time to leave. For example, if I park along a road that runs north and south, and hunt east of the road, I know I only have to walk west to find the road at the end of the day. That way, I don't have to interrupt my concentration and check a compass all the time. Of course, there are places where you don't have a long straight line to refer to. That's when a map comes in handy. Other reference points are lakes, power lines, fences and rivers.

If you don't want to bother with a compass or map (you should keep them in your daypack anyway), then hunt in a drainage that always keep you oriented. For example, if a stream has a road or trail next to it, you can hunt high up on each slope all day and simply descend to get to the stream at the end of the day. You might also hunt where landmarks are obvious, but be aware these might be obscured in bad weather, or if it gets dark and you aren't out of the woods yet.

Don't make the mistake of hunting in snow and assuming you'll simply backtrack to get out. You might strike someone else's track and become confused, or the snow could melt if it wasn't very deep to start with and the day warmed up. Also, new snow could cover your tracks.

If you want some reference points to temporarily mark your route, use plastic flagging, but remove it when you leave. You should use it only to mark specific locations you can return to, but don't be afraid to use it in a way that allows you a degree of confidence.

Be especially alert as to your route out if you're hunting until the last minute of shooting light. If you're far enough away from a road, you might be walking out in the dark. As I've said before, always carry at least two small flashlights with fresh batteries and an extra package of batteries.

Be familiar with daily weather reports and hunt accordingly. Be extra cautious during periods of prolonged rain or bitter cold. Carry survival gear in your pack and wear adequate clothing. There's no reason to get in trouble on your elk hunt. Use your common sense and be prepared for anything, because practically anything can happen in the elk woods.

Scouting

Elk country being what it is, a big part of scouting is looking over the terrain and vegetative features as well as the legal boundaries of your hunting unit. You're apt to be hunting a vast chunk of steep, perhaps roadless landscape. Your quarry lives in a herd, which may be anywhere in an enormous area. Other than becoming familiar with the boundaries and general layout of your unit, your scouting mission is to locate either those elk or escape areas where spooked animals may go when hunting season starts. Ideally, it would be wonderful to pattern a bunch of elk before opening day so you'll have a firm plan as your season begins. Unfortunately, if you're hunting public land in one of the many national forests in the West, as most elk hunters do, you'll have company from other people. The disturbance caused by hunters setting up camps, cutting

firewood, driving every road and doing their own scouting probably has an instant reaction on elk herds. The animals will abandon Plan A—their daily routine—and shift to Plan B—the stress/escape option. All your efforts before the season opens at patterning animals might be in vain once the elk are savvy to a new season that's about to begin.

Unless you're hunting deep within a chunk of national forest land, with no chance of venturing onto private property, it's a good idea to know precisely where you can or can't hunt. Scouting is important here. This is especially true if you're hunting private land and must strictly adhere to property borders. Virtually all private lands containing prime elk country are off-limits; to hunt them you often must pay a staggering trespass fee or hire an outfitter who has leased the ranch. In some states, private land does not have to be posted—it's incumbent on the hunter to know on whose land he or she is hunting. In states where laws require private land to be posted, signs must typically be placed no more than

a specified distance apart from each other. A splash of orange paint on a fencepost is a legal posting notice in some states. Take great pains to accurately identify boundaries during your scouting efforts. If you wander onto posted private property, you'll risk an embarrassing encounter with the law as well as a hefty fine, even if you were honestly confused as to property lines.

Of course, a good updated map is mandatory, unless you're thoroughly acquainted with your hunting area. You can buy Forest Service or BLM maps that indicate land ownership, roads, contours and other features. For even more detail, obtain topographic maps, since they show a much more expanded version, as well as important features such as springs, pack trails, two-track roads and other landforms that help you plan a hunt with more vision of the country. You can get Forest Service and BLM maps from the respective district offices, and topo maps can be purchased from sporting goods stores or through the mail. And thanks to the Internet, topo maps and aerial

photos are now available (many for no cost) with the simple click of a computer mouse.

A map is useless for scouting unless you know what to look for. If you haven't been to the area you're going to hunt, you're essentially peering at a strange piece of paper showing roads, streams, valleys, mountains and other features. Your two primary objectives are determining a camping spot and a hunting spot. Unfortunately, many hunters figure it's a good idea to do both at the same location, so they haul their camp to the edge of a meadow that was heavily used by elk. Notice the word "was." That's past tense, because the elk immediately move to parts unknown once you've been spotted, and they'll likely hear and smell you from a distance.

I recall an instance where I'd discovered a fresh wallow with a well-defined trail leading to it from the nearby forest. Prior to the season, I watched from a distance and saw a nice bull headed to the wallow about an hour before dusk. To confirm this activity and establish a pattern, I watched one more time and saw him again. He showed up at almost the exact time he had before. The wallow was located next to an old two-track road—to get to it by vehicle you had to drive over a rickety bridge that looked like it wouldn't hold a grocery cart, much less a pickup truck. I always parked at the bridge and walked the mile to the wallow.

I was confident this bull would wear my tag, and intended to wait near the wallow. You could have knocked me over with a feather, however, when my flashlight showed a set of fresh tire tracks leading to and across the bridge. I quickly hiked up the old road and saw a tent pitched within 10 yards of the wallow. The hunters were still in bed, as indicated by some serious snoring, and I left, disappointed and frustrated. That bull would be safe, at least near the wallow, because he'd surely detect the intruders and switch to Plan B.

STARTING FROM SCRATCH

When using your map to formulate some basic hunting strategies, look for a spot within a few miles of where you generally want to hunt, and be sure the regulations allow you to camp there. Now you need to roll up your sleeves and figure where exactly where you want to hunt, or to start your hunt. Remember, I'm assuming you're a total stranger in the area, and have no clue about the local elk herd. No one can find elk on a map, but you can make some educated guesses. What you're looking for are places elk like to be in, but essentially you're looking for starting points. Everything may change once you actually visit the area and get a first-hand look.

It's no secret that elk like feeding in big grassy meadows (parks). Forget those near main roads, unless you're in a limited-entry unit with few hunters. Otherwise, count on other hunters seeing those accessible, visible animals. Check the back roads, and take hikes where you can look at mountain slopes out of view of a road. Meadows surrounded by heavy timber are preferred because elk have nearby security cover. Many maps are color coded, showing forests in green and grassy meadows in white. You can locate these meadows without ever visiting the area.

Assuming that elk may change their habits prior to the opener because of human disturbance, you want to find escape areas. Look for places as far off the beaten track as possible, away from ATV and pack trails. Steep slopes are often selected by elk for escape cover, especially if they have heavy timber and blowdowns. Elk prefer topping over ridges on saddles, which are low spots on ridges. By checking map contours you can locate saddles for use as ambush sites.

Elk need to drink water. This fact won't help you if streams are common, but in some arid spots, livestock water holes are commonly used. Your topo maps often show you water holes as well as natural springs and seeps.

Try to get to your hunt unit at least 2 days before the opener. Set up camp and then begin scouting. Your objective now is to look for elk, as well as sign, and the all-important escape cover and routes. Remember, and it's worth repeating, if you locate a herd of elk near a road, other hunters may have them located as well. Always have another plan in mind, and try to locate as many feeding and bedding areas as possible.

Becoming familiar with the general layout of the land is essential since you may need to switch strategies and areas quickly due to competition from other hunters. The most consistently successful hunters are those who scout incessantly, learning every tiny piece of the place they hunt. To be savvy about elk, you must first become acquainted with their backyard. The more you know, the better your chances of scoring.

Many years ago I was hunting in an unfamiliar area and I didn't have time to scout. It was a blustery day, and a blizzard rolled in, dumping 3 inches of fresh snow. As I walked, I suddenly spotted two elk in the timber. All I could see were legs, and the elk were running full bore, obviously intending to make it to the next county. Then again, maybe they'd stop and offer a shot.

Following their hot trail was a piece of cake. I slipped along, easing through the trees and looking for what I hoped would be an elk. In fact, I had only a bull tag, and hoped that one of those animals would be wearing antlers.

The tracks didn't offer me any optimistic hopes. They were splashed in a straight line, going through and over every obstacle in the way. I had an idea these elk might not stop, but I maintained my careful pace just in case. I came to the edge of the timber, and entered a huge sagebrush valley that swept away to the horizon. The elk had run straight into the open, and were nowhere to be seen. I was frustrated because of my unfamiliarity with the country. Had I known the sagebrush expanse was there, I could have easily sprinted and cut the elk off at the edge of the forest. Instead, I'd been dutifully following the tracks, totally ignorant of the situation.

Common Types of Elk Sign

TRACKS, which measure 3½ to 5 inches in length, are often found in the soft soil around wallows and streams.

DROPPINGS take the form of 1-inch-long pellets when elk are browsing, small soft piles when they're grazing.

RUBS, made while practice-fighting during the rut, announce a bull's presence to other elk.

My mood wasn't improved when my companion told me the two elk were enormous bulls. He was sitting in a Jeep parked at the edge of a road when the elk almost ran into the vehicle. This is a classic example of the importance of knowing the country you hunt, and scouting it before the season.

When you scout, two clues are most obvious and are easy to see—evidence of foraging and droppings. Being grazers, elk nip off grass, and you'll easily see this telltale sign in mountain meadows. Droppings look like those of deer, but are half again to twice as large. Droppings may linger for years, depending on the climate. Fresh droppings glisten, and are soft to the touch. If droppings are on top of snow, you know they were deposited since the last snowfall. If the temperature is cold, the droppings are warm and the season is open, get your trigger finger ready—the quarry is close by.

Tracks show up plainly in moist soil, but may be indistinct in arid country. Elk tracks look like oversized deer tracks, but they're much larger. A mature bull's track is considerably larger than a cow's, but a spike or raghorn may have a track equal in size to a big cow. Don't make the mistake of confusing elk tracks with those of cattle or moose. Novice hunters often do that. Cattle tracks are more rounded and don't have the typical deer shape. The hoof prints of moose are much longer and narrower than elk.

WHEN ENOUGH IS ENOUGH

Keep your scouting efforts minimized, since you don't want to spook elk out of the country. Once you've located fresh sign, back off and scout more earnestly when the season is open and you're carrying a rifle on your shoulder. Try to pattern animals with as little disturbance as possible.

Most hunters don't have the luxury of scouting a new area for a day or two immediately before their hunting season. If you can't schedule that time, perhaps you can take your family on a summer vacation in the general area and have a look around. Even a few hours in the woods is worth it.

I remember an elk hunt in another state that held plenty of promise. I was going with a good buddy, but neither of us could arrive before the evening prior to the opener. As it turned out, I had a business trip months before the hunt in a city nearby, and I rented a car at the airport, took a couple days after the business was done and drove to the unit.

I located several areas to camp in, realizing the prime spots would probably be taken when we arrived for the hunt, and spent the rest of the time just roaming the woods with a map and compass. I looked for sources of water, possible feeding areas and escape cover. Since elk season was far off, there wasn't much sense in patterning animals. All I wanted to do was get a feel for the land.

I'm not very fond of showing up in a strange area in the dark and hunting in the morning. I always feel I'm not holding a full deck, and don't like the idea of being handicapped in the sense that other hunters are competing for the same elk. It's always prudent to stack the odds in your favor any way you can. Scouting offers that edge.

WALLOWS are made by bulls using their antlers to scrape out large depressions in soft ground.

BARKED TREES (inset) are the result of elk chewing on aspen trunks.

GRAZED GRASS is often found in mountain meadows used frequently by numbers of elk.

Physical Conditioning

Given the nature of elk country and the need to transport a heavy animal if you're successful, your physical condition is of paramount importance. It's a good idea to have a physical examination if you're over 40 or have some premature ailments. Your heart and lungs will be working overtime, as will your legs and back.

The best way to deal with your heart is to have your doctor give you a thorough exam. An EKG, a treadmill test and whatever else is suggested should be taken. You might need to shed some pounds and get involved in a good exercise program. Because it takes some time to condition yourself properly, see your doctor long before your elk hunt.

Your lungs are best conditioned by exercise and eliminating habits that aggravate them. If you smoke, you will no doubt feel the effects of tobacco when you hike and climb in the elk woods. It's up to you to determine how important it is for you to be in top shape. If it's a priority, quitting smoking is your only option. Tobacco also commonly causes people to cough. This is a no-no regardless of what type of game you're hunting, but is especially noticeable when you hunt elk because of higher altitudes and less oxygen, as well as the extra demands placed on your lungs.

Your legs will be profoundly impacted by the constant walking and climbing, and your back will be put to the test if you have to carry elk meat. Again, exercise and perhaps weightlifting will put you on the road to good health. Your doctor is your best advisor as to a diet and an exercise program, because each person is different. What works for your pal might not work for you.

I'm not much for disciplined exercise. I've tried it, but can't maintain it consistently as a habit. My wife works out on a NordicTrack every day, but it's just not for me. I quickly get bored, perhaps because the routine is monotonous, and I quickly tire of it. I get some good workouts by walking my Lab in the hills around the house. There are few level spots near my home, so my legs and lungs get some good exercise. I also enjoy cutting firewood for home use. With the proper permits, I cut dead trees in the nearby national forest and saw them into firewood lengths in the woods. Wearing my back brace, I carry each chunk to my pickup, which may be a distance of 100 yards or more. Then I split the wood when I get it home, a little each day. In the summer before hunting season, I work with wood at least 3 days a week to achieve some consistency. As I mentioned, exercise is a personal matter; you must choose some form that is appealing.

Jogging has been popular for a long time, and requires some dedication and a certain allotment of time. If jogging is too strenuous or unappealing, simply walking a mile or more every day or so is better than nothing. Once you're into it, you can increase the distances you walk and pick up the pace a bit. I've learned that walking around a high school track, for example, isn't nearly as effective as walking where you must climb and descend hills. Anything that helps simulate the conditions you'll meet on an elk hunt is good for you. What you don't want to do is to go on an elk hunt with absolutely no exercise unless you'll be hunting out of a pickup and don't intend to do much walking or packing meat. Even so, you should always anticipate the unexpected. Many hunts have a way of turning out differently than you thought, especially elk hunts.

I don't do it much anymore, but I used to ride a mountain bike well before hunting season each year. This is great exercise, and fun because you can ride to different spots every time and see new country, even if it's around your suburban neighborhood. Riding a bike is a superb way to condition yourself; it strengthens most of the muscles in your body as well as your respiratory system.

Back pain plagues many people, and is especially worrisome on an elk hunt because of the need to deal with heavy objects and bend and twist your body. If your back causes you problems, like mine does, do the specific exercises that help strengthen it. A doctor can advise which work best. Back problems are also aggravated if you're overweight, which is an excellent reason to go on a diet.

When my back goes out, I'm normally laid up for a few days, and then it slowly heals. When it goes out, it's always because I've bent over and twisted around at a bad angle, or picked something up the wrong way. Once, my back went out while I was on a wilderness hunt. I simply bent over to get a sock off the tent floor and saw stars when the sudden pain hit me. I laid in my sleeping bag for 2 days; it was all I could do to get up to make nature calls. Unable to ride my horse, I found a stout stick and used it as a cane to assist me in the long and arduous walk out. I now wear a back brace whenever I expect to be lifting or carrying heavy objects. It's a simple, inexpensive fabric brace sold in any large department store such as Walmart or K-Mart. I carry the back brace in my daypack so it's always available.

PACKING the antlers and meat of an elk is a major undertaking, especially in deep snow. Proper physical conditioning before the hunt is an absolute must before attempting such a task.

One aspect of elk country that may cause a health problem and allows for no preparation beforehand is altitude sickness, commonly known as *acute mountain sickness* (AMS). According to research, about 30 percent of humans suffer from AMS when they visit high elevations, whether they're skiing, snowmobiling, hunting or sitting in an alpine restaurant enjoying dinner. The typical remedy is to immediately descend from the high altitude. Relief should be almost immediate, but in extreme cases there could be some long-term effects. Symptoms include headache, nausea, fatigue, lightheadedness and dizziness.

Far too many people take elk hunting lightly and refuse to condition themselves. You won't realize the mistake until you're wheezing your way up a steep mountain, or experiencing a new pain that might be terrifying. If you're seriously overweight and are going on a horseback hunt, your outfitter might not have a horse to sustain your weight. Chances are right at 100 percent that a profoundly overweight person won't travel very far from a road, which decreases his chances of getting close to an elk.

Another problem caused by overweight hunters is injury to the horse. Because large people tend not to balance well in the saddle, their weight may cause sores on the horse's back. Once a horse is sored it should not be ridden again until it heals, which can take several days.

If you aren't in good shape because of age or a chronic problem or ailment, or if you simply haven't conditioned yourself for whatever reason, do yourself a big favor and plan your hunt according to your capabilities. Hunt in rolling country rather than in steep terrain, and pace yourself. This is especially true if you're following a guide who will likely be much younger than you and in top condition. If hunting with pals, have them drive you to a ridge and drop you off where you can slowly meander your way. Hunt to a lower road where you can be picked up at the end of the day. Consider carrying a two-way radio, but only to request assistance if you put an elk down—never use the radio to help you locate an elk. This is illegal in some states and always unethical.

Tragically, some hunters come home from an elk hunt with a serious medical problem caused by the strenuous exercise, or worse yet, they arrive home in a body bag. It happens every year. Make your hunt more enjoyable and successful by seriously considering a physical conditioning program after a visit to your doctor. Everyone is better off for it, including yourself, your family and your friends.

Hunting Techniques

Glass & Stalk

If you take a cursory look at typical elk country, you'll see heavy stands of timber growing on steep slopes. Grassy parks are usually woven into the forest mosaic. A novice hunter accustomed to hunting whitetails in the back 40 may be totally baffled by the western landscape. Many people have no idea where or how to start hunting, and simply park their vehicle and walk around the mountains.

GLASS AND STALK BASICS

The elk hunter's day should begin with an intensive glassing session. The idea is to locate elk in the meadows before they drift off toward bedding areas in the heavy timber. Since elk feed most actively during the night, they're most commonly observed during the first and last minutes of daylight. By taking advantage of this basic behavior pattern, you can make visual contact with the quarry, and then formulate a plan to immediately intercept or stalk those animals, or plan a strategy for later in the day. Distant animals may be too far away for you to make a stalk when you spot them in the morning.

The chances of observing feeding elk are best in areas where hunting pressure is light. Large numbers of hunters cause elk to become even more nocturnal; the animals typically leave the meadow feeding areas long before the first glimmer of light. Not all the elk will be out of visual contact, however. You'll just have to work harder to find them.

Feeding areas aren't always in open glades and parks. Chances are good that animals are foraging in a small pocket or basin off the beaten track. A big mistake is to take a cursory look at a spot that traditionally has elk, and seeing none, head for another slope, drainage or ridge top. I've found this to be

GETTING A GOOD SHOT at an elk is the reward of careful glassing and stalking.

true in the elk woods: Your chances of locating animals improve considerably as you distance yourself from the routine patterns of other hunters. It's common for people to take the easy way out. Perhaps you're looking at a large area and see no elk. Rather than being tempted to move on, drop down a steep slope or climb a high ridge where you can observe the area from a vantage point not used by other elk hunters.

Once, when I was hunting during a general Colorado season, I glassed a big clearing that almost always held elk early in the morning. No animals were present, and I knew the clearing tapered off behind a stand of spruces and then opened up into another big glade. It was shaped sort of like an hourglass, with half of it completely out of sight from my location. In order to see the rest of it I had to descend a slope, climb around to a finger ridge and, finally reach a promontory offering a superb view of not only that clearing but many others. It took me 45 minutes to get to my destination, and I was rewarded with the sight of a dozen elk, including a decent bull. They were just drifting off into the timber, and I wasn't able to move within shooting range before they disappeared. I wouldn't be able to hunt them in late afternoon, assuming they reappeared in the same clearing, because I had to help a buddy cut up and carry out an elk he'd taken the day before. That project would last until dark.

I was back at the hourglass clearing the next morning, and I hastily made my way through the dark woods with my flashlight. I stayed inside the timber until just enough gray light from the impending dawn allowed me to move without the flashlight. Then I eased to the edge of the timber where I'd seen

BINOCULARS allow you to pick apart the dark shadows of the forest. With the naked eye (inset) the bull above could easily be missed. With binoculars, however, you can readily distinguish the bull from his surroundings.

the elk the previous morning, and saw absolutely nothing but an empty meadow. I'd had many experiences like this one before; just when you think you've got a bunch of animals figured out, they do something else.

I figured one of three things happened: 1) the elk were spooked by hunters the previous evening and had moved to a new area; 2) they moved naturally to a new area, as they often do for no apparent reason; or 3) they were somewhere close by, but out of sight. I decided to stay in the spot for another hour, because prime time was almost gone and I wouldn't be able to check out a new spot before the sun pushed elk into the timber.

I was there for 10 minutes when I heard a cow chirp from the other side of a small ridge. Watching intently, I spotted a single cow walking over the ridge. Soon another followed, and then the rest—10 in all, followed by the bull. He walked within 75 yards of my location, and I took him with an easy shot. I

never would have scored had I not known that much of the clearing was out of sight from the traditional glassing area used by most hunters.

To locate animals in the morning, it's imperative you follow the elk's schedule, which may be quite foreign to your own. That means you need to be in place in the mountains in the dark, long before morning's first glow. To do this you must be willing to leave camp in the dark, forsaking the wonderful warm sleeping bag and hitting the trail in the cold, snow, wind and otherwise miserable conditions you're apt to find in the mountains. You should have scouted the area to have some idea where elk are living, and your mission now is to spot those elk and quickly plan an ambush or stalk before they move into the timber. Once they reach the woods, the party is usually over as far as glassing is concerned. They're gone for the rest of the day.

If you know the country and have a good idea where elk prefer to bed, you might second-guess the herd and try to cut them off at the pass, so to speak. During a hunt in Wyoming, I saw a herd of elk in the distance, and there was no way I could get within shooting distance because they were already headed for the timber. With the wind in my favor, I swiftly moved to a point where I believed they were headed. A small ridge with clumps of lodgepole pine and aspens offered just enough visibility to allow me to get a shot if indeed they passed through that spot.

I was ready to call it quits an hour later, but suddenly I heard a twig snap. A 5x6 bull was slowly slipping through the brush, offering a target whenever he walked into one of the tiny openings. The bull quit walking and stayed in one spot, as still as a statue. All I could see was one of his antlers and his rump; the rest was hidden. I had an idea he might have heard or seen something amiss, and decided to try just a peep on my cow call. As soon as I called he took two steps and looked at me. A hole in the brush the size of a basketball opened up perfectly behind his shoulder and I took the shot. The bull ran 40 yards and collapsed.

When you reach your vantage point early in the morning, settle in and make yourself comfortable if you intend to look at a lot of country. In some places, you might have only one or two meadows to look at, in which case you'll want to "hit and run." This means you check out the meadows and if no elk are present, you hustle around the other side of the ridge or to another vantage point and look some more.

Before glassing, sit where you have a good view, and support your binoculars on your knees to steady them. Slowly observe the target area, and don't make big sweeps. Instead, pick out a small spot and glass it intently, then look at another spot adjacent to it, and continue until you're satisfied that you've thoroughly covered it. Then do it again. Many times animals move out of the edge of brush where they can be spotted, or away from shaded areas that previously hid them.

Perhaps the biggest mistake hunters make is careless glassing. The common attitude is that if an elk isn't seen on the first pass with the binoculars, it isn't there. That's an unfortunate conclusion, because many times elk are there to be seen, but go unobserved because the hunter is too hasty or too impatient. It should also be remembered that even if animals

Bushnell spotting scope

are in the open, weather conditions may be such that the elk can't be spotted with the naked eye, no matter how good your vision or your ability to spot elk are.

There's another reason for wearing binoculars, and that's for safety's sake. If you're carrying a scope-sighted rifle but no binoculars, you'll be tempted to use the scope to identify a shape or movement in the distance. Should the object be a human, you'll have committed the most serious violation in firearms safety—pointing a gun at a human being.

If you're intent on a big bull, or if you're hunting in an area where a legal elk must have a certain number of points, you'll need a close look at the quarry. A spotting scope is a good choice, and allows far more magnification than standard binoculars. Not many years ago, a spotting scope was literally a pain to carry because of its weight and bulk; nowadays you can purchase a lightweight, compact unit that is easy to pack. A spotting scope is virtually useless without a tripod mount. Trying to steady one on a rock, a log or a walking stick is always a poor second choice. You can buy small tripods that easily stow in your daypack.

Once you've located elk, you have two options, remembering that time is now of the essence. You may have just minutes before the elk head out of the opening and into the timber. If they're close enough, your first option is to quickly slip through the woods and stalk close enough for a shot. If they're too far away, or are just about to reach the safety of the timber, your second option is to plan an ambush later that afternoon. Unless they're disturbed by other hunters during the day, chances are good they'll return to feed in the same opening, probably using the same route and trail they traveled on in the morning.

A dilemma might present itself if the distant elk you've spotted are in a place unfamiliar to you. Once you leave your vantage point, you may not be able to see that particular meadow from another spot, and it may be impossible to locate it. You may find yourself deep in strange woods with no idea as to the location of the original meadow.

A map and compass or GPS unit is the answer. Before you leave the area, get

your map out and plot the meadow's location as carefully as you can.

Follow a bearing as you travel, or use the coordinates from your GPS unit. The latter is far more hunter-friendly, allowing you to slip about and hunt without always having to keep track of a bearing or referring to a map. But be aware that a GPS unit is a high-tech gadget that can fail. Always use your compass as a backup.

As you stalk, be always watchful of wind direction, and plan your route so you're downwind of the elk, even if it requires a tedious, more lengthy approach. Your clothing should be constructed of a fabric that is quiet when in contact with brush. Cheap nylon and even some expensive garments are extremely noisy, especially those with water-proof exteriors. Since sound might betray your movements, try to stay on trails as much as possible. Don't be deluded into thinking that snow offers quiet walking. It does, but only under specific conditions, such as when the snow is powdery, or just after a fresh snowfall. If snow thaws and freezes, it will crunch louder than dry autumn leaves. In that case, it's virtually impossible to stalk elk. The colder the air temperature, the louder the noise made in snow. It's virtually impossible to sneak up on an elk when the temperature is 0°F or lower.

THE FINAL APPROACH

As you make your final approach to where you think the elk are, the objective now is to spot a single animal in the herd to confirm their presence, since they might have moved when you were stalking. Several eyes, ears and noses offer a

GLASS AND STALK HUNTING requires you to use the terrain to your advantage. Because this bowhunter's outline is broken by the rocks behind him, he won't be spotted by elk.

formidable defense. In order for you to penetrate this protective zone you must be exceedingly stealthy, taking great pains not to be spotted as you move. Remember too that in most elk states, you'll be required to wear hunter orange during the firearms season. This doubles the need to keep a low profile, which may involve crawling commando style.

If you spot the elk without them seeing you, your next task is to locate the desirable animal. If you have a cow tag, you'll likely try for a young, dry cow with no calf at her side. Cow hunts are meat-gathering expeditions; therefore, a mangy old wet cow is not usually the hunter's choice. Look the herd over and watch their movements. You can often determine which cows are mothers by observing the calves. If you take a wet cow, incidentally, the calf will survive with no problem. During the fall, calves are fully weaned and are immediately adopted into the herd if their mother is lost.

Trying to spot the herd bull may take some doing if he's accompanied by several cows. Generally, he'll be lighter in color, and may be slightly away from the herd. If your glassing efforts haven't allowed you to get a good look at his antlers from a distance, you'll need to carefully try to size him up with your binoculars. This is a difficult task if he's in cover or screened by trees.

Your approach will be much easier if the cows and calves are talking. They'll often make chirping or mewing sounds when they feed or walk about, giving you the advantage of pinpointing their movements by listening. (This is extensively covered in the chapter on calling, p. 88.)

If you've been spotted by a cow, stay where you are and don't move. Don't make the mistake of easing down into cover while the cow is watching. If she doesn't quite have you figured out, remain stationary. If you disappear in the brush by easing low, she's apt to really spook. Your only hope here is that she'll decide you're part of the landscape and go about her business. If she barks, the game is over. All you can do is to look hard for the target animal and take your shot. Her barks will quickly alarm the herd, and you can be sure they'll depart immediately.

In the event the elk were too far away to stalk when you spotted them in the morning, consider waiting them out in the late afternoon. Again, check the wind direction and move from the downwind side. Get positioned at the edge of the clearing where you can find cover behind a tree or bush. Stay well away from the route you expect the elk to take, unless you're hunting with bow or muzzleloader. In that event, you'll need to try to find the specific trail they're using and set up close by.

Invisible Elk

I learned a lesson many years ago, one I'll never forget. My pal and I were heading back to the truck after a miserable 10-mile hike around the mountains. We had seen no elk, and no fresh tracks, despite snow on the ground. At one point we stopped under a big pine tree on the edge of a big clearing to munch on candy bars. We were whipped and looking forward to getting out of the woods.

We casually looked across the clearing, but nothing stirred. We'd seen elk there in the past, but this time it was barren. We were preparing to leave when my buddy took a look out across the clearing with his binoculars. He gasped in surprise and told me a dozen elk were feeding on the far side of the clearing, in a small patch of sagebrush. I looked, but couldn't see anything with my naked eyes, and raised my binoculars.

And there they were—a dozen elk, including a raghorn bull that would fit my tag nicely. Because it was snowing and a misty fog had settled in across the clearing, those elk might have been underground as far as we were concerned. They matched in perfectly with the brush, and were so obscured by the poor weather they were impossible to see without glasses. I might add that my buddy has outstanding "game eyes." He's the type who spots animals long before anyone else in the hunting party.

We worked toward the elk with the wind in our favor, and ended up shooting the bull. We scored because my pal used his binoculars.

How many times does "not seeing what's there" happen to hunters? Of course, there's no way to know. I suspect every hunter, whether he's a novice or veteran, has missed seeing elk that were there to be seen because he didn't use binoculars.

Before making the decision to position yourself in late afternoon near a meadow far from a road, consider two very important requirements: Can you find your way out of the woods in the dark, and can you dress an elk by yourself in the dark? It's possible the quarry may show up during the last few minutes of shooting light, and darkness is a certainty. If the answer to either of these questions is no, then look for elk located closer to a road or trail, or hunt with a companion. Having a pal along makes sense, not only for safety and assistance in field-dressing an elk, but also in watching a large meadow. It's possible the elk may appear anywhere; having more than one hunter is a good plan.

Calling

Calling elk is often considered a mysterious technique that must be mastered in order for it to work. Truth be known, the caller's skills at deciphering an elk's intentions and mood, and responding accordingly, are far more important than making the perfect call. Most modern calls offer a superb rendition of the real thing, and you don't have to be a champion elk caller to produce the correct sounds.

TYPES OF ELK CALLS

Before state-of-the-art elk calls appeared on the hunting scene, we used homemade versions constructed out of a garden hose, willow stick, or short length of pipe. The sounds that emanated from those primitive calls were tinny, shrill notes sounding nothing like the real thing. But wonder of wonders— they worked.

My favorite call was one I made from piece of willow. An old-timer taught me the procedure. I wish I still had the call, but somewhere it disappeared. Several notches on it indicated the bulls it had duped. Then along came the so-called diaphragm call, which is attributed to Wayne Carlton, a southerner who migrated to Colorado and stayed. Wayne, whose company manufactures calls, discovered that the diaphragm, which was used exclusively for calling turkeys, could also make both bull and cow elk sounds.

This discovery did not go unnoticed by other call manufacturers and elk hunters. In just a few years,

more than a dozen companies produced the call, making subtle changes and variations. The call itself is about as large in diameter as a golf ball, but is horseshoe shaped. It typically has a metal or hard plastic rim, to which is attached a thin piece of latex. Calls come in many colors and size variations, though they must fit completely into the mouth, where they are positioned next to the roof.

Therein lies an inherent problem. Insertion of the call into the mouth may produce a gag reflex, not unlike that experienced when a doctor sticks a tongue depressor in your mouth to look at your tonsils. Because of this undesirable reaction, many hunters are leery of the call, and look to other "external" type calls that are simply blown in the manner of a whistle.

To add more realism, resonance and depth to the call, the caller blows into a grunt tube. This tube is

typically nothing more than a length of auto radiator hose about 1 to 2 inches in diameter. Modern tubes now come in camo colors; some have bulbous features producing a throatier sound, and many have a mouthpiece rather than being a chunk of hose built into the call.

For the sake of realism, the diaphragm call used in combination with the tube seems to be the choice of experts and is the most common type used in major elk-calling events.

While the bugle of the bull is the first and sometimes only thing that comes to mind when hunters think about elk calling, cow and calf sounds also play a major part in elk communication. The vocalizations made by cows and calves were never considered useful in hunting techniques until the mid-1980s, when it was discovered that imitating those animals

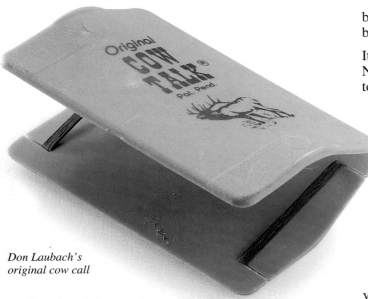

Don Laubach's original cow call

produced positive results. Don Laubach, a veteran Montana elk hunter, revolutionized elk hunting when he produced the first cow call.

Laubach lives in Gardiner, Montana, a unique town literally bordering Yellowstone National Park. Because of its location, elk live in and around Gardiner much of the year. Don watched and listened to cow elk with interest, and, being a hunter, had the notion he could duplicate their sound and use it as a hunting tool.

I've known Don for years, and I listened with some skepticism when he gave me a prototype cow call to try. Mind you, there were no calls like it in existence; this was hallowed, untested ground. I tried the call for a couple years and was amazed at the results.

In 1986, I wrote an article for *Outdoor Life* magazine called "Elk-Hunting's Newest Secret." From that point on, Don Laubach's name became a household word among elk hunters. He began manufacturing cow calls, and found a willing, eager audience ready for this unprecedented technique. As was the case with Wayne Carlton's discovery of the diaphragm call, Laubach's brand-new idea was quickly accepted by the call industry. In just a few years, a dozen companies were producing their own versions of cow calls.

When and How to Call

Bulls bugle from mid-September to early October, when most hunters are not afield. Exceptions are bowhunters, who have exclusive bugle seasons in every major elk state. Elsewhere, muzzleloader hunters may hunt in some selected areas during the rut; so can modern firearms hunters in some wilderness areas and limited-entry units in several states. For the general-season rifle hunter, however, many seasons begin in mid- to late October or early November, after the elk

breeding period is over. For the most part, efforts at bugling elk are in vain at that time.

It's possible to hear bugling long after the rut, even in November and December. This is usually attributed to a cow that wasn't bred when she was in estrus during the breeding season. When she returns to estrus again, bulls get fired up and carry on, but normally won't respond well to calls.

For those fortunate enough to hunt elk during the rut, few other hunting opportunities can match the beauty, ambiance and aesthetics of the elk woods in September. Aspens are at the peak of their colors, rivaling the accolades given to New England's fall foliage, and the western weather is typically perfect, with blue sky days, crisp and refreshing sweet mountain air, and elk music echoing from canyon to ridge. Many hunters view the taking of an elk as a bonus, and are perfectly delighted at simply being in the woods during those magical days.

Though calling in a bull during the bugle season is often considered the quintessence of elk hunting, hunters more often go home empty-handed than with an elk, and not because of a lack of animals. Bulls are no pushovers, despite the claims of a few writers who describe a furious charge by a screaming bull after only one attempt at calling.

A bull makes a call that rises in pitch and then typically ends with three or more grunts. The call is commonly described as covering four notes, but there are many variations. Some bulls begin their call with a high note, dropping down to low, throaty tones. I've heard bulls wheeze, snort and bray like jackasses. It's virtually impossible to describe bugle sounds in print; the best way to familiarize yourself with elk calls is to rent videos on the subject.

I believe the term "grunt" is inappropriate. To me, a grunt is a sound made by a pig or a bull moose. I think the elk's sound more closely resembles the whine of a puppy. For the sake of conformity, I'll use the now-accepted term. Sometimes bulls grunt without bugling, and sometimes their grunts number far more than the standard three or four that hunters typically hear.

At times, bulls may bugle like there's no tomorrow. Once, when I was hunting with Jack Wemple, a Montana outfitter, we were deep in a draw, headed for a bugling bull up on the opposite ridge. To get to him, we had to cross a rushing river with some very tricky footing.

Suddenly we heard another bull behind us, up on the slope we'd just descended. This bull was bugling non-stop, and grunting and carrying on for all he was worth. Jack and I stood and listened, and immediately noted that the first bull had quit, but the newcomer was still talking incessantly.

We decided to try for the second bull, and huffed our way back up the mountain. I was motivated in that harried climb only by the bull that wouldn't quit bugling. In fact, he sounded more intense than ever. Jack and I continued the tortuous climb, panting as we went. It was obvious the bull was traveling around the slope, and if we could get up to the level he was on in time, he might walk straight into us. It would be the perfect ambush.

And that's exactly what happened. After crawling several yards in dense huckleberry brush, I eased up to see the bull standing there staring at us. Instantly he turned and made a leap, but I was able to snap my rifle up and put a bullet into his spine.

Jack and I couldn't understand why this bull was so vocal, but close inspection seemed to explain it. There was a deep hole in his head squarely between his eyes, no doubt gouged by the tines of a rival bull during a battle. We deduced that this bull was either very mad or very hurt. Either way, he had sounded off like no other bull I'd ever heard in my life.

A cow's call is commonly called a chirp or mew because it sounds like a bird or kitten. Indeed, people unfamiliar with cow sounds may mistake them for a bird in the woods. Calves make similar sounds. Some hunters believe the calf's voice is higher pitched, but I haven't observed much of a consistent difference between a cow and calf. While cows and calves are credited with making chirping sounds, mature bulls do this as well.

GRUNT TUBES are used with diaphragm calls (inset).

CALLING ELK is easiest to learn by watching a good video on the subject. Have your call in hand while watching the action and try to duplicate the sounds made by the experts.

Some hunters claim they can determine the size of a bull by his bugle. That's absolutely absurd, since enormous bulls may make reedy, whiny sounds, and small bulls may sound like the King of the Mountain. No two bulls sound the same; each has its distinct voice.

Bulls refuse to come to a call for many reasons, and if they do come, they'll often "hang up" out of sight, refusing to approach any closer. Some elk hunters

believe bulls hang up due to the proliferation of high-tech calls in use these days. They argue that bulls are growing accustomed to these artificial sounds and either won't respond at all or hang up before the hunter can get a shot. It's also often said that bulls seldom bugle as much as they used to because of the presence of more people in the woods during the rut.

It's obvious a bull won't come to a caller if the elk thinks it's bogus—no surprise there. But bulls can make such awful, untypical sounds that the caller would have to be terrible to warn a bull. Moreover, the bull is probably alerted to the conditions surrounding the call—the location of the hunter, as well as the betrayal by human-type noises and wind currents.

Many hunters make their calls from heavy human-traffic areas—along trails and roads, near camp and along ridge tops where other hunters walk. Often those calls are preceded by a vehicle door that's just been slammed, or a human voice, or another factor. To avoid this dilemma, simply get off the beaten track and call as close to a bull's location as possible. Drop down into heavily timbered slopes where no pack or vehicle trails exist in the bottom. Hike

Bowhunter calling from the "jungle"

but a good percentage of herd bulls are uncallable. A satellite bull is a solo animal with no cows and would very much like to have one. But he's apt to turn you down because he isn't looking for a fight, which is what you represent with your bugle call.

There are some tactics you can employ to work up a bull's temper and encourage him to respond. You can try being aggressive by running toward him, bugling as you go and breaking branches. Of course, you must be downwind of the bull at all times, and behind screening cover.

Another calling trick is to try to get between the bull and his cows. This can be difficult, depending on terrain and vegetation, but if you can, your bugle call will likely produce a mean-spirited bull at your front door in a jiffy.

Bulls often respond if you scrape a stick loudly across the bark of a tree, and break branches loudly. This represents a bull that is having it out with a sapling, which often occurs several times a day. This limb-breaking and thrashing often entice bulls within earshot to run over to see what animal is making the commotion.

If a bull bugles back to your call, it's best to wait a few minutes before calling again, unless he's hot. You can tell he's hot if he bugles several times. In that event, answer his call one for one. Otherwise, play it slow and easy and be ever-watchful for a silent sneak. Many bulls approach silently; you'll see movement in the vegetation before you hear them. Often an elk circles downwind to pick up your scent.

into out-of-the way pockets and basins where other hunters are less apt to go. Bottom line here is the need to outsmart not only a bull but other hunters. You can blow on a call and make the perfect sound from a ridge overlooking the nicest elk country in the world and not get a peep from a bull. But descend down into the jungle and try again, and you might very well get an answer. Getting in his backyard often does the trick.

A bull might also refuse to answer because he thinks you're another bull, which is precisely why he won't respond. A herd bull already has his harem, and logically retreats when he hears another bull, since his mood is set on romance instead of battle. In order to gather the cows in the first place he likely had to steal them from another bull or at least defend them continually. Some herd bulls are aggressive enough they'll indeed investigate a hunter using a bugle call,

Your calling location is extremely important. If you're in an area with fresh sign and you believe elk are close, don't call until you're totally ready. A bull may come in quickly, before you're prepared for a shot. Pick a spot where you have good shooting lanes, especially if you're bowhunting. Be sure you have a busy backdrop to break up your outline such as tree branches, brush, downed logs or other forest matter. Don't stick out like a sore thumb in the open woods and never skyline yourself on a ridge top.

A bull's bugle can be deceiving. You'll likely think he's much farther away than he really is. If you can hear him grunt after the bugle, he's probably no more than 200 yards away. If he decides to come in fast, he can cover that ground in seconds. Always expect him to show up anywhere, anytime.

If a bull you're calling hangs up, you might try running away from him and bugling as you go, bolstering his ego and encouraging him to chase you. The wind, however, may give you away, since he may run into your scent. Another option is to team up with another hunter. The first hunter takes a stand close to the bull and remains silent. The partner stations himself well in the rear, at least 100 or 200 yards away, and bugles. If all works out, the stubborn bull advances toward the caller, unaware the quiet hunter is in his face.

USING COW CALLS

Cow calls are effective in calling both herd bulls and lone bulls that won't come to a bugle call. Many herd bulls can't resist adding another lady friend to their harem and dash to the caller for a look. The solo bull is lonesome, and his natural wariness is temporarily clouded when he hears a cow, enticing him to check her out. Lone bulls aren't necessarily small bulls intimidated or whipped by bigger herd bulls. They can be older bulls that simply have lost their dominance and vigor, and their antlers would make trophy hunters drool.

Most hunters carry two or three cow calls and one or two bugle calls. It's important to remember that if you spook an elk with a particular call, it's likely he'll never respond to that call again. He's learned the little nuances and subtleties of the call, which is why you should switch to another.

Elk-calling videos show the best learning techniques, and it's a good idea to observe someone who knows how to use the call well. If you can't master the diaphragm call, all sorts of other calls on the market allow you to simply blow into a tube. Be selective when shopping for one, because some don't allow you to make the grunt sound.

Cow/calf calls can be made with the diaphragm, a tube, or a "bite and blow" call. These are simple sounds to make, requiring far less effort than a bugle call. Since cows and calves communicate year-round, you can often call them to your position after the breeding season or at least get them to chirp back, revealing their location.

Another variation is to use the call occasionally as you're walking through timber when elk are bedded in the daytime. If you're away from trails and logging roads and in the underbrush (which is where you should be), you'll undoubtedly be making noise. This is to be expected, because it's impossible to slip silently through heavy cover. Remember, you should make nothing more than quiet, natural noises caused by walking through brush and snapping small twigs. Loud clothing rasping against brush betrays your presence to elk, as will metallic sounds made by your gear, buttons, Velcro fasteners, and other bells and whistles we seem to carry around. The human voice is a big no-no as well, and it's surprising how many people talk loudly in the woods.

When the elk hear you coming, they'll be at full alert, listening, watching and smelling. If you blow a cow call occasionally, they'll think you're another elk. What this does is allow you to approach much more closely before they spook. With luck, you'll be able to spot them first, but that's typically unlikely. Once they've homed in on your location, they're apt to see you long before you know they're around.

Here's where you produce another sound on the call. By making a loud, piercing chirp, you can often stop spooked animals from running. Upon hearing the sound, they'll likely stop and stare, giving you an opportunity for a shot. I believe this works because the sound is similar to that of a bark. A cow barks because she's alarmed, and when that happens, all the other elk in the herd immediately stare at the barking cow. When the alarmed animal has identified the danger, she'll run off, bringing the entire herd with her.

During a Colorado hunt, I was heading back to the truck during a fierce blizzard when I saw a bunch of elk running hell-bent for the next state. They were 300 yards out, which was much too far for my liking, so I set my rifle on my shooting sticks, and blew the cow call as sharp and loud as I could. Every elk stopped on a dime and stared, which was what I was hoping they would do. The raghorn bull in the bunch never knew what hit him.

Calling is a technique that varies with every hour of every day. Experiment as much as possible, and closely observe elk habits. Remember, the call itself is secondary. Understanding what elk are saying and why they behave as they do is far more important than being a world-champion caller.

Stillhunting

Of all the hunting strategies for big game, stillhunting is no doubt the most challenging. The term itself is misleading, since stillhunting implies that one is being still while hunting. In reality, the hunter moves at a snail's pace, taking a few very slow steps, then being still for a period of time. All the while, the stillhunter becomes part of the woods. He blends in with the foliage, moving with the wind in his favor, and uses every one of his senses to locate the quarry before it spots him. Generally, stillhunting includes looking for sign as well as the actual animal, and it has a surprise element—you don't know animals are present until you actually see them standing or bedded. If you locate tracks and follow them, you're no longer technically stillhunting, you're tracking (p. 104). If you spot a distant elk and slip up to it, you're stalking (p. 83). That's why stillhunting is so difficult. You're pursuing the unknown, and won't know it until you suddenly spot it.

Stillhunting for elk is especially tough because of the vastness of the country as well as the rugged, densely foliated terrain. The hunter must be able to recognize subtle sign and know when to pick up the pace or slow down, depending on the clues left by animals. Walking too slowly may not allow you to cover enough ground; walking too fast may cause you to miss seeing sign, or to flush elk prematurely.

STILLHUNTING BASICS

The first requirement in stillhunting is to know what an elk looks like under poor light and in heavy cover. That might seem too academic, given the size of an elk, but the quarry easily blends into cover. The chocolate head and mane and tan body offer superb camouflaged coloration. Nothing can substitute for first-hand learning in the woods, and veteran elk hunters have stumbled into and spooked countless elk by not spotting them first. They always will, and, of course, so will the novice.

I recall one of my first elk hunts when I really didn't know what to look for. While I had seen plenty of elk before, most were out in the meadows and clearings, and I had yet to come face to face with one in the timber.

I was sneaking through the forest with a light breeze in my face and light snowflakes filtering through the canopy overhead. Suddenly I smelled something odd, sort of like a barnyard smell associated with cattle, but I couldn't be sure. I'd heard that elk could often be smelled at a distance, but this was new to me. I stopped and waited, looking through the underbrush with my binoculars.

Moments later I saw something moving. It was just a small motion, but enough to notice in the almost-calm woods. For a few seconds I couldn't tell what I was looking at, and then I realized it was the head of a cow elk. She was chewing her cud, and I'd seen her mouth moving.

Since I had only a bull tag, I settled in to wait and watch. Nothing else was in view, just the cow. Slowly I settled down to the ground, where small shrubs screened me from the elk. I crawled commando style to a point where I'd have another view. I peered over the top of the brush and saw three more cows, but no bull.

The cover ran out, and it seemed my only choice was to wait. Shooting light would end in an hour, and I knew the elk would be up on their feet soon, headed to a feeding spot. Twenty minutes later a cow got up, stretched and nibbled about in the understory. Soon another rose, and in 10 minutes I saw six cows and calves. They turned and headed away from me, and then I saw more elk in front of them that had been hidden from my view. For a moment I saw antlers on one and brought my rifle up. Try as I might, I couldn't get a clear shot. For the few feet that the bull was visible, a cow was either in front of or behind him. The herd meandered off, and though I circled and tried to set up an ambush, the wind changed and betrayed my presence. I heard the elk crash away in the timber.

I was disappointed, of course, but at the same time satisfied that I'd been able to sneak in on a herd of elk. I proved to myself that stillhunting is a very effective technique, but it must be done with great care and caution.

Another time I was hunting with two pals who had drawn a tag in a limited-entry unit. I knew the area well, but they lived across the state. A week before the season I'd located a herd of 50 elk, including a fine six-point bull and several spikes. I had a hunch they'd be there when the season opened, because few people knew that elk inhabited the spot.

Sure enough, after my pals arrived and got settled in camp the eve before the opener, we found the elk exactly where I'd left them the week before. My friends were as excited as they could be, and couldn't wait for the opening hour the next day. Their attitude was contagious, and I was about as excited as they, even though I hadn't been able to draw a tag.

DEEP SNOW makes for excellent stillhunting. Look for elk in areas with heavy cover and be ready for a quick shot.

Long before dawn we awoke and were on the road. I dropped my pals off a mile from the elk and they worked toward them in the dark. I noted with approval that no other vehicles were in the vicinity. Hopefully we had the elk to ourselves, if, of course, they were still where we thought they'd be. In order to minimize our disturbance I remained in a thick patch of junipers while my pals worked their way to the elk.

I heard a shot a few minutes after shooting light, and was pleased that everything went off perfectly. Then a second shot, and I knew that both my friends had scored. But then there was a third, and a fourth, and a fifth. Something was wrong.

By the time I reached them they were walking around staring at the ground, disappointed and definitely not "happy campers." They'd drawn straws to see who would shoot at the big bull, and that hunter would take the first shot. The second would take a spike. Evidently the elk were farther off than they thought and they misjudged the range.

I looked up on the slope of a nearby mountain and saw the entire herd making their way up through the sparse junipers. I could see the big bull and the same three spikes that had been with the herd ever since I discovered them. All were healthy; none showed signs of being hit.

I knew about where they going, and was aware of a an old road on the other side of the mountain leading to the top. We quickly jumped in a vehicle and headed up. We parked a half mile away and hastily worked along the ridge. A very steep, rocky sidehill on the other side of the mountain fell down to a large river. On the other side, where we last saw the elk, there was a very thick forest of junipers and pinyon pines. The elk weren't on top, and I guessed they'd be in the thick forest, already bedded.

My two pals had their work cut out for them. To get to the elk, they'd have to still-hunt like they never had before. I waited on a big bluff overlooking the forest while they entered the trees with the wind in their favor.

Two hours passed, and I began to wonder what was happening, when suddenly I heard a shot. Then one more. Then silence. I stayed rooted to the spot, because I didn't want to be walking around and get

STILLHUNTING often brings you into contact with more than one elk at a time. Before you move to take a shot at a particular elk, make sure there aren't other animals hid by brush or in the shadows (photo above) that could betray your presence.

in the line of fire if they needed to finish off a wounded elk.

Fifteen minutes later my pal walked into a clearing and gave me a thumbs-up sign. Through my binoculars I could see a grin from ear to ear. As the story unfolded they slipped into the trees and slowly looked for the elk, moving just a few feet a minute. Finally, they spotted a bedded cow, and they dropped down prone on the forest floor. By slowly maneuvering about, they were able to locate the big bull and a spike. But there was a problem. A cow was bedded directly behind the big bull, and my friend couldn't shoot. They waited more than an hour, but still none of the animals changed positions. Luckily, the wind remained in their favor the entire time.

Deciding to take a chance, one of the hunters whistled softly. The bull immediately got to his feet and presented a clear shot. My friend fired, and so did the other—at a spike he was watching but couldn't shoot until both shots were coordinated.

My pals had done something that took a lot of patience and skill. They worked their way into a

herd of elk without being seen, smelled or heard. This was a superb example of textbook stillhunting.

Stillhunters who are extremely cautious can often slip into a herd of elk if conditions are perfect. I've done it a number of times, but it was always an exceedingly difficult task. By "perfect" conditions I mean a steady breeze that doesn't change direction. This is not often the case; many times I've seen the wind blow from every direction over the course of a half hour. Another factor is the composition and density of the forest. If the forest floor is cluttered with blowdowns and thick patches of shrubs, such as huckleberry, it may be impossible to see animals or to make the final move to get into shooting position after they're spotted.

Elk almost always choose an evergreen forest to bed in, even if they spend much of the night in aspen stands or patches of scrub oaks. By knowing their affinity for evergreens, you can pay special attention to these places if the landscape offers a mix of cover. Obviously, a mountain with nothing but evergreens won't have any starting points, but a mountain with aspens on the slopes and Douglas fir on the ridges gives you an idea as to where to focus your stillhunting efforts.

Being humans, our brains seldom stay focused on the primary objective when we hunt—looking for an elk. Too many distractions confuse the goal. We may find ourselves thinking about a problem at home, on the job, or with our kids, or a myriad of other subjects keeps us from intently focusing on our surroundings. A raven flapping away high overhead, or the yipping of a coyote, or the presence of a bear track—these and other sights may also distract from the task at hand. The result is often an explosion in the timber made by a bunch of elk busting from cover. You might want to kick yourself for not paying attention, but it's the price you pay for losing the power of concentration. Of course, plenty of elk are positioned where you cannot see them, no matter how skilled you are. But a certain percentage of them should have been spotted but weren't because of the hunter's error.

Stillhunting success begins with your clothes. You must foremost be comfortable, so your mind isn't complaining about being cold, or wet, or hot. Wear appropriate clothing suited to the weather, and carry extra apparel in your daypack, if necessary. Wear a good hat, gloves, and warm, waterproof, broken-in boots. The latter are extremely important. A big part of the stillhunting technique is moving quietly; your boots assist you in accomplishing that if they fit well and are easy to walk in. Quiet clothing is a must. Choose quiet outer garments. Wool is a great choice, and there are countless types of synthetics that do well, but many do not. Even expensive, state-of-the-art clothing nowadays may be noisy and essentially worthless to the stillhunter. To check the quiet-quality of a jacket or trousers, run your fingernails across the fabric and listen. A loud, scratchy sound identifies it as a poor choice for stillhunting.

Even with soft, quiet clothing, you might still be unable to walk quietly because of the heavy cover. No hunter, regardless of how savvy he is, can move stealthily through a spruce blowdown or doghair patch of lodgepole pine. You will make noise, but remember elk make noise, too, though they have the advantage of slipping along indistinct trails you and I can't see. The noise you make must be natural—brush slowly swishing by your clothing, a cracking branch, or a bit of snow dislodged from a fir bough. What won't be tolerated by elk are human sounds such as metallic noises made by gear, a Velcro pocket being opened, a cough, a sneeze or a human voice.

The latter should be obvious to anyone, whether they're experienced in the elk woods or not, and it constantly amazes me how many people I hear at a distance. They carry on normal conversations, and quite often shout. The human voice is a confirmation to all elk within earshot that humans are nearby. The animals might not leave, depending on their tolerance of people, but they are aware of human presence. And as a result, your stillhunting efforts are far more difficult.

Let's present a scenario in which you're sneaking through the woods, unaware that a half dozen elk are bedded 50 yards away and hear you coming. They can't smell you, because the wind is in your favor, and they can't see you because of the cover, but they're at total alert, ready to bolt any instant. You can't see them either, and you continue your stroll, when suddenly they flush in a blur of enormous bodies and images thumping through the forest. They don't go quietly, but raise bedlam, busting branches as big as your wrists, and tearing new passageways in the thicket.

You have a couple of options. One is to let them go and remain quiet, hoping they'll settle down, whereupon you can eventually sneak up on them again. Another is to tear through the forest trying for a shot, which is usually foolish and always unsafe if your rifle contains a chambered round. A third is to stop them by making a sharp whistle with a cow call. This trick works amazingly well, but few hunters have tried it because the last thing you want to do when elk are busting away is to fiddle for a call and blow on it. Seeing is believing, however, and many hunters who try it are converted. To be effective, you must have quick access to the call. By carrying it around your neck on a string, you can grab it instantly. Blow the call with a loud, crisp sound, and be ready for a shot. Don't be surprised if the fleeing elk stop in their tracks and stare.

Occasionally the spooked elk splinter off in two or more groups, becoming separated by the confusion of their hasty exodus. A strategy that often works to gain you a shot in this situation is to entice them to you with the cow call. Since the elk naturally want to regroup back into one herd, and they do it by vocalizing, your imitation of a cow will likely arouse their interest. Blow the call softly, but sparingly. If the ruse works, the elk will believe you are part of their fragmented group and slowly begin easing to your location. Blow the call each time a cow answers, but wait several seconds after her call. This should be a calm interchange, because the animals are casually trying to locate each other. Many times spooked elk travel a short distance from where they were disturbed, and stop to listen and look for danger. If they didn't smell you, but caught just part of your outline, they usually calm down after a couple hundred yards or so, which is well within earshot of the cow call.

Another use of the cow call is a random vocalization as you routinely move through heavy cover. I like to blow the call softly every time I make a loud noise, or every couple minutes. This reassures unseen elk within earshot that all is well and that the sounds they're hearing are made by other elk instead of a human. This ploy allows you to get much closer than normal. Of course, the herd is alert, and every elk is staring in your direction because of the unavoidable noises you're making in the underbrush. Your chances of spotting these elk first are slim to none, but remember that when they eventually spot you, a sharp note on your cow call may bring them to an immediate halt.

Not all elk woods are festooned with leafy obstacles causing you to make noises as you squeeze and slip through the cover. Many forests are more sparsely vegetated, allowing you to ease quietly. The speed at which you should move is an individual preference, but I like to walk rapidly until I locate fresh sign telling me elk are about. Fresh tracks and droppings tell me to shut down the quick walking and begin a slow, methodical search of the woods around me.

If you walk too slow as soon as you leave the road or trail without considering the lack of fresh sign, you might hunt all day and never be within a half mile of a living, breathing elk. The enormous country you must search must be evaluated as to its potential, and then you must make an earnest hunt. On the other hand, if you move too fast, you might blunder into elk, but that's the chance you must take. You're working the odds here, and sooner or later you're going to catch the quarry flatfooted if you work hard at stillhunting. This is an intense pursuit, and may end up a failure rather then success, but that's the nature of the technique.

WHEN AND WHERE TO STILLHUNT

Choosing the time of day to stillhunt is an important decision, since animal behavior varies widely. Most hunters choose to check out the meadows and openings at first shooting light, hoping to locate feeding elk. If the early morning efforts are unfruitful, hunters then either take to the woods and hope to find elk in the timber, or head to camp and give it up until the last couple hours of shooting light, when elk begin moving again. The worst possible time to stillhunt is at high noon, give or take a few hours, since elk will likely be bedded and in their most unapproachable stronghold. If you head for the deep woods when elk are still active, moving from feeding to bedding areas and vice versa, stillhunting becomes more positive, since you may hear or see walking elk before they spot you.

In some elk woods where forage grows in the forest, elk may not move for long periods, and may travel only a few hundred yards during an evening's feed-ing. These elk are quite at home, and if a small seep or spring is handy, they may remain there for weeks. These are the toughest elk to approach, because they're so familiar with their micro world they can detect danger quickly and be out the back door before you even know they exist. Because they remain in one area so long, droppings, tracks and feeding signs are unusually abundant. These should tip you off that you're in or close to an elk's home, and you'll have your work cut out for you to spot this animal.

If you want to pick the best place to stillhunt, having the highest odds of holding elk, look at your map and locate the nastiest piece of woods you can find as far from a road as possible. Remember, the quarry is often at high alert and in maximum escape mode. They'll take cover in areas where they're least disturbed. On the other hand, stressed elk may prefer to hide in patches of cover close to roads simply because hunters overlook those spots and never bother to step a foot in them. Choosing a stillhunting spot may be a roll of the dice, but your scouting efforts should have gained you some insight to elk habits.

Once I was driving along a highway through a pinyon juniper forest when I saw a dead elk calf lying next to a road, evidently hit by a vehicle. I was amazed, because the nearest elk I knew about lived 15 miles up the highway in the forest. I continued to drive, and then realized this low-elevation forest might be a fertile new hunting area no one knew about. But if anyone else saw that dead calf, they'd be on to the elk population too. I turned around, drove back to the calf, dragged it a few yards below a guard rail so it was out of sight, and reported it to a game warden as soon as I got to a phone.

I returned to the spot a couple weeks later, wanting to satisfy my curiosity. I walked into the forest, and discovered an astounding number of fresh elk tracks, most of them a mile from the highway. A couple months later when hunting season opened, I was back in the area, and found it to be a superb place to stillhunt. The pinyon and juniper trees offered just enough visibility that I could see in front of and around me reasonably well. I took two elk in the area, and finally word got out. Since the spot was public land, other hunters moved in, and essentially scattered the elk to where they were difficult to locate.

There's a special satisfaction in taking an elk one-on-one in his domain. That's what stillhunting is all about. You might fail most of the time, but the occasional success makes it well worth the effort.

Driving

Don't let this technique confuse you if you haven't tried or heard of driving. No, it doesn't mean riding around in your pickup truck looking for an elk, but purposely moving animals to hunters waiting on stand (standers). The elk are actually being driven by moving hunters (drivers).

The basic fault with this strategy is that you never drive animals where you want them to go; instead, you drive them where they want to go. This is true with deer, elk or any other animals you're trying to drive, but it's exceedingly more difficult with elk because of the nature and size of the environment in which they live. Trying to make a drive through a huge area of thick timber is largely a waste of time. If you're extremely lucky, the plan might work and elk will run by a stander. Otherwise the elk run somewhere else where there are no standers, or they'll hole up and stay in the timber, refusing to be driven.

Before starting any drive, the first order of business is to hunt a place where you're reasonably sure elk are living. That place by necessity must be small enough to allow the plan to work. The drivers should be able to cover the likely spots, and the standers should be able to see most, if not all, of the escape routes. Try to find spots bordering large clearings, sparsely covered evergreen slopes, or fairly open aspen forests. Ideally, an area of 30 to 100 acres is good, since drivers can slowly walk about and cover much of it, and standers can watch the borders. If the area you're hunting is an island of timber completely surrounded by clearings, so much the better, since the elk have no choice but to run out into the open. That is, if the elk come out in the first place.

Once you've determined the location of the drive, it's a prudent idea to sit down with the members of your party and talk about safety. Drives are inherently risky because people are concentrated in a relatively small area, and their locations are usually unknown to all members of the party. By all means, require everyone to wear a hunter-orange jacket or vest and a hunter-orange hat, even if the state you're hunting in doesn't require it.

Next, decide who will drive and who will stand. Select these hunters according to their physical condition and hunting experience. Generally, the standers have an easier time of it, requiring a walk to their stand location or perhaps being dropped off

STANDERS should find ambush locations well hidden from approaching elk. The best spots give standers a good view of the landscape and feature a solid rest for accurate shooting.

from a vehicle. Hunters who are elderly or out of shape, or have physical problems should stand. Consider as standers any unskilled hunters who might be prone to getting turned around if the drive is in heavy timber. Drivers often can't see or hear each other if the cover is large or thick and the wind is blowing.

Make sure the drivers know where the standers are located in the event a driver has a shot at an elk. Some hunters prefer the drivers not carry firearms at all, for safety reasons. The standers should likewise be aware they must have a safe background before shooting at an elk.

There are two types of drives: noisy and silent. In the noisy variation, drivers break branches, shout, bang on tree trunks with stout sticks, bark like dogs, sing—whatever it takes to frighten elk. The belief here is that elk are so unnerved by the racket they'll flush from their beds and head for the next county. An advantage is that all members of the party—standers and drivers—can keep track of all the drivers; thus they can pick and choose their shots much more safely. But so can the elk, and they are much more evasive since they can pinpoint the drivers' positions.

The silent drive may be more effective in moving animals since they're confused by the stealthy movements of people close by and might be more prone to flee. The disadvantage is that hunters are not aware of the locations of other people in the party.

TIPS FOR SUCCESSFUL DRIVES

While it's obvious that standers should watch open areas, it's important to have someone watch any fingers or extensions of timber connecting two stands of trees. Like savvy whitetails, elk often choose to escape in cover instead of breaking into the open.

Drives should never be done if you suspect elk are bedding in an area and are naturally going to feeding areas you know about. The last thing you want to do is interrupt this pattern, since it's far easier to waylay moving elk than to dig them out of the brush. A drive may be okay if you have only a day left to hunt and need a last resort, or if the elk are moving strictly at night. In either case, you have nothing to lose.

I know of a party of hunters that knew where a bunch of elk were bedded, but the hunters were too impatient to figure out where the animals were feeding. Instead, they put on a drive in the timber that was far too big to work effectively. The elk never came out during the drive, but stayed in the forest. That night, the entire elk herd left and were never seen again during the hunt.

Another time I was in an elk camp that was seriously overbooked with hunters. Instead of the six hunters that routinely made up a party, there were 14. The outfitter's only option was to put on drives every day because he didn't have enough guides to go around. Of the dozen drives that they tried, only one bull was taken, a raghorn that ran toward a stander.

I seriously doubt any elk were in most of the places being driven, because I tried still-hunting in several of them afterward, and I saw little, if any fresh elk sign. Unfortunately, the outfitter was simply eating up time and going through the motions of making this ill-fated hunt look good.

Drives can involve anywhere from two hunters to a dozen or more. Once I hunted with a pal from the East who had zero experience hunting elk. I put him on stand in a narrow finger of firs that connected two large timbered areas. With the wind at my back, blowing toward the elk I hoped were there, I slowly slipped through the timber, zig-zagging back and forth, and trying to penetrate as many possible hiding spots as I could.

I saw some sign, but never heard or saw an elk as I moved about. When I was a few hundred yards from my pal, I heard him shoot. I walked over and saw him smiling over a fat spike bull. He was pleased as punch, and related how the bull and three cows ran straight at him after I routed them from the timber.

The wind is often overlooked during drives. I think hunters believe the chaos of the moment overrides an elk's senses, and the animals will simply burst out of the woods and run toward standers. That's an unfortunate assumption, because spooked animals are paying close attention to what their noses tell them. Elk often make an about-face if they smell humans in front of them, and may never come out of the timber during the drive. Much of their behavior depends on the degree of danger they feel.

I've been on a number of drives where horses were ridden by the drivers. This is extremely effective if the timber allows horses some freedom of movement. A skilled driver can rout elk and stay with them just long enough to move them out of the forest. An unskilled horseman is better off not trying to take part in a drive. Horses are easily confused in the timber, and may balk at being directed through brush and limbs. The result might be a rodeo with the rider bucked off and seriously hurt, or the rider might be scraped against a tree by a nervous horse, or scratched by sharp limbs. It could be dangerous to be charging around in the forest with ever-present branches that could poke out an eye.

Some years ago, I was hunting in Colorado with two pals. One of them killed an elk on the opener, and we were taking turns driving on horseback. One of

us would stand, while the one who killed the elk and the other who hadn't scored put on the drive. It was my turn to stand, and I sat in a small, open aspen draw with my horse tied up in the brush above me. It was a lovely day, and I was about to drift off to sleep when I heard a twig snap in the forest. I came to alert, and heard the unmistakable thump of a hoof striking a log. If my assumption was correct, elk were moving in the timber, and would break out far below me.

I sprinted 100 yards and quickly rested my rifle on a log. I didn't hear anything, and I figured the animals had stopped to listen for my pals who had spooked them. Sure enough, the herd of elk busted out of the timber, a five-point bull and five or six cows. A pair of cows ran out into the aspens, and the others milled about in confusion. The bull was only 60 yards away, and I took him with a single bullet behind the shoulder.

My buddies showed up 5 minutes later, and said they hadn't seen the elk, but heard elk crashing through the timber in front of them. It was a perfectly executed drive.

The next day we put on another drive and ran a bull by our other pal. We scored 100 percent, with three nice five-point bulls, and we took them on heavily hunted public land.

There are two types of frightened elk—lightly spooked elk and terrified elk. The former may linger within the area being driven and not come out, or sneak out through cover. Terrified animals may dash into an open clearing and literally run through camps, over tents, and around trucks and other human obstacles to get out of Dodge.

If you're on stand and elk are running, blow sharply on your cow call and be prepared for a quick shot, since the elk often stop in mid-stride and stare at you. Unfortunately, if you're like most hunters, the excitement of seeing elk cancels your thought processes, and you'll likely forget to blow the call. This is especially true if you haven't tried to stop elk before and aren't confident that the call works. Have the call handy before the drive starts. Put it on a log where you can grab it, or better yet, hang it around your neck on a lanyard.

Elk drives are techniques best done when all the factors are clicking nicely. They're iffy at best, and shouldn't be counted on as the primary strategy. Try them when all else fails, and hope for the best. What you don't want is to run elk deeper into the backcountry. They're tough enough to hunt without making them even more elusive.

Hunting from Blinds

Though elk hunting is generally considered a mobile activity where you constantly hike and travel through big country, there are situations that warrant hunting from a blind. Obviously, before doing so you must have some idea of the quarry's behavior pattern.

TREESTANDS

Much elk country is unsuited for treestands because of the nature of the timber. Whereas in the whitetail woods a treestand increases visibility and puts you above the quarry, the evergreen timber composing most western forests doesn't allow you to see much, if anything, from an elevated perch. In fact, it's usually easier to see elk from the ground than a high stand. Spruce and fir trees, for example, have thick boughs growing from the ground up. To use a self-climbing treestand, you'd have to prune away all the branches from the ground up the desired height. And even for a small strap-on stand you'd have to clear enough branches to climb the tree and place the stand. Either way, you'd still have to clear shooting lanes, since adjacent trees block visibility as well. This chore can be done, but visibility would still be quite limited. Of course, you'd need to obey rules that pertain to cutting green trees and limbs wherever you happen to be hunting.

There are places where treestands would work well, such as quaking aspen forests, where the tree trunks are "cleaner" (as in whitetail woods), and you can scoot up in a treestand and have good visibility. A treestand would work along the edge of a clearing, or in sparsely vegetated woods, but their value, again, is questionable because the elk hunter must be able to travel according to animal movements.

There are some situations where treestands can be effective, primarily for bowhunters who are afield before the rut. Stands over wallows and waterholes are productive if well-used trails are located and watched. Otherwise, most bowhunters are afoot, using calls to get within range of elk.

GROUND BLINDS

Hunters can best ambush traveling elk by taking cover in a ground blind. Here again, there's a vast difference between ambushing elk and whitetails. Elk have an enormous area to roam, and may leave the country at a moment's notice. For that reason, the hunter who prefers hunting from a ground blind must be flexible, having several locations to hunt from depending on the movement of elk. And these locations may need to be several miles apart.

Ground blinds can be sophisticated works of art carried in a backpack and set up with tubes, rods, fabric, etc., but most hunters simply fashion them from whatever natural material is available. A few spruce or pine boughs piled high enough to hide a hunter usually suffice, but in reality there are enough deadfalls and clumps of brush in the western forests that an elaborate blind isn't necessary.

Elk may not notice a fresh blind as a whitetail would, since a deer lives all its life in a relatively small area, and is familiar with every detail in the environment. An elk is so nomadic it might not recognize a new structure. That being the case, you don't need to set up blinds in advance of the hunt for elk to become accustomed to, except in places where elk have a comparatively small home range and move very little.

Setting up a blind near a waterhole or wallow may require a subtle design that doesn't alert animals accustomed to coming in for a regular drink. When selecting a location, consider the prevailing wind direction, which is usually from the west in elk country, but pay attention to mountain thermals as well. Typically, nighttime breezes blow from high to low elevations, and reverse during the day.

If you're hunting with a centerfire rifle, you can locate your blind well away from the waterhole, but bowhunters and muzzleloaders must be in much closer. It's usually best to set up well away from a waterhole and close to a trail, because you might be too obvious when close to the water unless adequate cover is available. Be alert when elk are approaching. At times they'll slip in slowly, checking out the area before moving in, and at other times they'll run in as if there's no tomorrow.

Using a blind near a feeding area is another effective technique, and you'll usually have plenty of cover to conceal yourself. Since meadows are primary feeding spots, and are generally flanked by heavy forests, finding a blind is simply a matter of hunkering down next to a deadfall or amidst a group of trees at the edge of the clearing. Some places, however, offer little cover around the forest perimeter, requiring you to fashion some sort of screen from branches and logs.

Since a meadow can be very large, perhaps up to a half mile long or longer, you should have done some homework to determine where to place the blind. Fresh sign denoting the most recent feeding spot is the best clue. Elk tend to feed in certain spots in large meadows, and then move on. If the animals appear 600 yards from your location, for example, and you're pinned down without the opportunity of making a move, you may be stuck until another day. For that reason, pick a secondary location you can sneak to if necessary. Determine your sneak route before the elk show up. Preliminary planning is always better than hindsight.

More than once I've watched a meadow from a blind, and had elk come out much too far for a shot, leaving me with the obvious necessity of making a hasty move. If shooting light is short, as is usually the case in late afternoon when elk finally drift out of the timber, your move has to be quick. Often, hunters become careless, forgetting about the wind, and may allow themselves to be spotted. Most of the time I don't have ground blinds set up, but use whatever is handy for screening cover.

There's a place in New Mexico I often hunt that produces dandy elk. I found a saddle on a ridge elk like to cross, and built a blind to the east of it, allowing a shot of about 100 yards. This location is ideal for the wind, since it typically blows from the west. It's also perfect for the early-morning sun, since it's at my back and in the face of the quarry. And since I hunt the spot with a muzzleloader, the distance is perfect.

I made the blind out of several logs and branches. It's backed up next to a huge fallen tree that forms a wall behind me, allowing me to move without being spotted, though there are spaces I can see through, giving me a 360 degree look at the forest around me. There are several places I can poke the muzzle through and find a solid rest.

It's fun to return to that spot every time I hunt the unit. Knowing I built the blind offers some sort of personal kinship to the area, and brings back memories of past successes. The familiarity adds a nice dimension to the hunt, and I always look forward to hiking up to the ridge to see if my little hideaway is still intact. Of course, any motivation I can come up with to climb a steep ridge is always welcome.

Tracking

To a deer hunter, tracking an elk might seem to be an easy proposition. After all, you're following a big animal that no doubt leaves a large impression as it walks. While that's basically true, it's the only easy part of tracking because, as you've read countless times in this book, elk country is big. In addition, elk often cover great distances between feeding and bedding areas, and walk for many miles when they're migrating. In other words, tracking an elk is usually a rugged undertaking.

Snow is the finest tracking medium, which is good because you'll often find snow from early October

on in the high country. There are no guarantees, but the later you hunt, the better chance you'll have tracking snow, especially in the upper elevations. Even in Arizona's mountain country you can expect to find snow during the late firearms seasons.

I recall an Arizona hunt when 4 inches of fresh snow fell during the hunt. It rained where I was camped, since camp was at a lower elevation than the hunting area, but as we drove to higher country before sunup I noted with glee that the ground was suddenly white. The higher we drove, the more snow we found. By the time we parked the truck and headed into the hills, the snow had quit, offering the very best tracking conditions one can find. Every track would be fresh, just a few minutes old. There would be no guesswork as to a track's age. All I had to do was follow.

It took about a half hour to find tracks, and when we struck paydirt it appeared that a big herd of elk had just passed through a large patch of greasewood. At one point I heard cows and calves chirping, and they seemed to be moving just ahead of us.

Suddenly another bunch of tracks appeared, coming up out of a draw, and they joined up with the initial group we were following. This new set of prints made my heart leap. All were bulls, and it appeared there were at least a half dozen.

Focusing now on the bull tracks, we trailed them carefully. The tracks split up here and there as the animals wandered about in the brush, but always regrouped. There seemed to be no question they were headed in a specific direction.

Twenty minutes later, I heard a loud noise ahead and looked to see a bull lunge from behind a bush and run off. Suddenly another bull appeared, and another, until chaos took over, and I found myself trying to quickly decide on the best of the bunch so I could shoot. The elk were running separately and in different directions, making it tough to size them all up since they were in and out of view as they tore through the brush. Finally I got it sorted out and shot at a bull that was evidently confused since it was angling toward us. Evidently it was unaware of our presence and was running because the other elk were obviously badly spooked.

He was a fine bull elk, with six points on each side. I was especially happy because Arizona was one of the last elk-hunting states in the West in which I hadn't hunted elk. It took me 6 years to draw a tag in a very competitive lottery.

After field-dressing the bull, I looked around in the snow and discovered an elk track that took my breath away. It was the biggest print I'd seen in a lifetime of elk hunting. I don't believe I laid eyes on that bull in the confusion of the moment when they flushed, because if his antlers were anything like his track, then I'd have instantly been enormously impressed with his headgear. Of course, big tracks don't necessarily indicate antler size, but this animal was far and away much bigger in body size than the others, indicating he was probably older. Age translates to bigger antlers, and I'll always wonder how big that elk might have been. I will never forget the size of his track.

TRACKING BASICS

There are three basic ways you can find elk tracks. You can watch the elk making them in the distance, and then work your way over and start tracking when you locate their prints. You can also see tracks in the snow at great distances with a spotting scope or good binoc-

ulars in openings where elk have fed or traveled during the night (it helps to have the sun shining, since the tracks are tougher to spot in flat, shaded light). Finally, you can discover tracks as you routinely walk through the woods, which is the way I located my Arizona bull.

However you do it, you should prepare for a long hike. Animals casually moving back and forth between feeding and bedding areas offer the shortest tracking session, though they may travel several miles where hunter pressure is heavy. The longest tracking efforts are in pursuit of migrating animals, which may walk 10 miles or more in a single day or night. In between are the elk pushed by hunters that are headed for another spot within their home range.

Telling an elk track from a deer track is easy, because the size gives them away. An elk track (p. 76) looks like an oversized deer track. You'll know one as soon as you see it.

Though many "foolproof" methods exist to supposedly differentiate between a male track and a female (as in a spike bull and mature cow, which have similar-sized prints), there are no surefire ways. The suggested clues such as placement of urine, dew claw marks, drag marks and walking style have absolutely no credibility. The only absolute way to tell is to see the animal standing in the tracks. When you see a bull track, however, you'll recognize it instantly if you're familiar with a cow track. The difference in size is most obvious.

Tracking requires quiet clothing. Since you're apt to be in snow, you'll no doubt be wearing heavy garments. Beware of some of the inexpensive, synthetic waterproof jackets—they are often noisy. Wool is my favorite choice when hunting in snow. It's silent and keeps you warm even when wet.

Animals are acutely aware of sounds behind them. You must be as silent as you can, but if the snow is crunchy, you'll probably fail in your efforts to catch up to the quarry. Instead, make a big circle if you know the country, and try to intercept the animals if the tracks are fresh. If conditions are such that the snow has thawed and the temperature is bitterly cold, the snow will be so noisy that you'd be wise to abandon tracking. Instead try some other techniques where walking isn't necessary, such as watching from a possible ambush point near a trail or feeding area.

Contrary to popular belief among folks who don't spend much time in snow, it's a rare day when snow offers silent walking. As a rule, the colder the air temperature the noisier the snow is, unless you're walking in pure powder with no old snow or a crust underneath. Thawing snow on a warm day offers reasonably quiet walking. The very best time is to track when snow is actually falling. If you can find a fresh track, the accumulating snow gives you a minute-by-minute account of the quarry's position in front of you.

TIPS FOR SUCCESSFUL TRACKING

You can usually tell if a track is fresh if the edges are crisp in soft snow. If they're frozen, they're undoubtedly hours or days old. In powder snow, it might be impossible to tell, since snow falls back into the track and doesn't allow any comparisons. If the powder is deep, you'll be lucky to tell if a track is made by man or beast. That sounds implausible, and I'm sure some folks would be skeptical of a person's skills if they couldn't tell an elk track from a man track, but I can assure you it's true. All you need to do, if those conditions are present, is to plunge your foot into the snow near what you believe is an elk track and lift your boot out. Compare the look of each, and I'll wager you can't tell the difference.

Other clues might help you tell, such as urine or droppings that haven't yet frozen, or droppings on top of the snow, indicating they're as old as the last snowfall. Also, warm droppings will thaw snow under them, sinking a bit. You can also examine them to see if they're crystallized with ice. If the dropping is warm to the touch and the air temperature is very cold, unsling your rifle from your shoulder and get ready for a shot—your elk is very close ahead. This scenario is guaranteed to put you at total alert. Knowing an elk is just minutes ahead of you will increase your pulse and accelerate your brain waves. Try to keep calm. This is a poor time to get the jitters and come down with a case of buck fever—or in this situation, elk fever.

The time of day should tip you off as to what the elk might be doing. As a rule of thumb, I always assume elk are bedded within 2 hours after sunrise. This might not be true when it's cold and elk aren't being pushed around by hunters. The animals might be on their feet longer, nibbling away at forage. It's far easier to track elk that are meandering around and feeding here and there than bedded animals. For that reason, it's important to try to learn what elk are doing when you're following them. If the tracks straighten out and are on a trail of some sort, the elk might be getting ready to bed down. Be ever watchful of a suspicious color or shape in nearby cover.

If you spot an elk, immediately come to a halt and take stock of the situation. Slowly raise your binoculars to identify the animal you've spotted. If it's an elk that doesn't interest you, put your glasses to work and scan every square foot of the forest. If you haven't been spotted, move just a few inches very slowly, and glass again. Keep it up as long as the elk haven't become alerted to your presence. If you're discovered and the animals flush, use your cow call to stop them.

Always assume there are a lot more elk than you can see, because there usually are. Remember too that just because you're watching an elk that's looking in another direction, perhaps calmly chewing its cud, it doesn't mean another elk isn't staring at you, its eyes riveted on your every move. Everything you do at this moment must be in super-slow motion.

If an elk is indeed staring at you, stop what you're doing, except breathing. This is one time in your life you must be as immobile as a statue. Blinking your eyes can't be helped, but everything else can. The only way to calm down the suspicious elk is to pray—and to fool it into thinking the possible danger it perceived was just a movement that can be trusted. If your ploy works, the elk will resume chewing its cud, but may not take its eyes off you for a long, long time. You'll soon feel protesting muscles, joints and nerves, and if you simply can't take it any longer, slowly lower yourself to the ground and lay there for a half hour if need be. When you're ready to peek again, don't raise up to the position you were in. Crawl, commando-style, with all your body pressed to the ground, and slither off to another spot where a tree or bush hides you as you lift up. You must adopt the role of a cunning predator, such as a mountain lion moving ever so slowly, inch by inch, until it reaches a point where it makes three or four swift bounds to catch its prey. In your case, you move inch by inch, but only to identify the precise elk you want to put your bullet into, and usually from close range.

TRACKING allows persistent hunters to unravel the movement patterns of elk and eventually locate the best bulls in the area.

Tracking often offers hunters a false sense of security. Because they know the elk are just ahead, it's easy to be overconfident. Perhaps hunters move along too fast, or fail to properly glass ahead. Many tracking efforts end up with elk busting out of cover, or with the hunter failing to catch up to the elk at all. As a hunter, you'll be following big animals in big country, and you'll quickly learn they aren't pushovers.

While you progress along the trail, it's easy to lose concentration and fail to focus on the task at hand. That's especially a problem if you've been following tracks for hours and it seems the elk will never stop. You can't imagine where they're going, and you wonder why they don't bed down. This can be most frustrating, seemingly an exercise in futility, but you must remember the elk can't go on forever. Sooner or later they must stop, or at least slow down to where you might be able to catch up.

Be aware of the legal boundaries of your hunting area. If you have a tag for a limited-entry unit, you won't be allowed to leave it. Conversely, if you're hunting in a general hunting unit and the quarry enters a limited-entry unit, you must quit at that point. If you're hunting public land bordered by posted private property, be aware of the boundaries and don't step across them. It's terribly disconcerting to follow elk tracks for hours and suddenly see where they've left your legal hunting area. That's an aspect of hunting you have no control over.

Knowledge of the country you're tracking in gives you a major advantage. If you know where elk like to bed, you can leave the tracks and possibly cut the animals off before they get there. Many times you can use topography to your advantage as well. If you're aware of a promontory giving a vista far ahead, for example, you can go to it and look for the elk you're tracking in the distance.

Once I tracked a half dozen elk in fresh snow for 3 hours and couldn't seem to catch up. The trail wound about in a quaking aspen forest, and one of the tracks was obviously made by a bull.

When the tracks headed toward a ridge I knew was covered with Douglas firs, I cut crosscountry and got on the ridge, assuming the elk would bed in the firs. I eased up on the ridge, walked toward the edge of the firs, and saw the six elk headed straight toward me, walking in single file up the slope away from the aspens. One of the elk was a four-point bull, and I dropped him at 80 yards. They had no clue I was anywhere in their world.

Tracking often requires variations in strategy that allow you to put yourself into the best position to locate the elk before they locate you. Following a trail is the simple form of tracking, but there's often much more to it than that.

To me, tracking is an exciting way to hunt. There's no question the elk is obviously in front of you; the big question is precisely where. Every step you take opens up a new vista, new country to explore with your eyes.

Hunting the Late Season

Elk-hunting seasons may run from August through February, depending on the state and the management objectives for each herd. Typically, bowhunters pursue elk during the breeding season in September, though some states allow hunting in August and into October. Because elk are vocal and can be called during the breeding season, archers have the opportunity to hunt them at this time, since it's essential to be close to the quarry for a shot.

During this period, elk are on their summer ranges. In some areas, that might mean very high elevations in the backcountry and in remote or wilderness areas. The logistics in reaching these animals as well as getting them out can be formidable.

Later, usually in mid-October or early November, the general elk seasons begin for rifle hunters. Depending on the weather, elk may still be high in the mountains, or they could be migrating to lower elevations if deep snows come early.

At some point, if the winter is normal, animals complete the migration cycle and spend the winter in valleys, benchlands, high deserts and other low winter range areas. Obviously, this is the best of all worlds for a hunter who holds an elk tag when animals are seasonally accessible.

But there's a catch. By the time elk get to the lowlands, hunting seasons are usually over. Very few general seasons are held late enough to take advantage of the migration. Montana is a notable exception, with a 5-week general elk season extending to Sunday of Thanksgiving week, which is in late November or early December.

There have been instances in the past when early winter storms have occurred during the Montana general hunt. When that happens, and elk are on accessible public winter ranges, hunting can be incredibly good. During one such season in the early 1990s, Montana hunters took more than 1,000 mature bulls from a fairly small area, and most of these were within a mile of a road.

So how can you hunt elk late if the weather doesn't cooperate during the general season? There's only one way, and that's to draw a limited-entry tag offering even later hunting. Unfortunately, weather is still the major factor, and since weather is unpredictable, even special late seasons may be failures. Compounding the problem is the fact that enough snow might be present in the higher elevations to make access difficult if you need to go high to find elk.

If you're interested in a late limited-entry hunt, you can apply for tags in states with such hunts. It's possible that bonus or preference points might be available to help you draw a tag. Since these elk hunts are so popular, you can count on plenty of competition for tags.

Some of the best late hunts are adjacent to national parks where elk migrate out and onto public lands where hunting is allowed. The most famous is the hunt just north of Gardiner, Montana, and in the Gallatin valley near West Yellowstone.

These are very short hunts—4 days for bulls, 2 days for cows—beginning in December and ending in February. Colorado has some special late tags for animals migrating out of Rocky Mountain National Park, and Wyoming has late hunts in November and early December for elk coming down from the east portion of Yellowstone and some high wilderness country.

Of course, obtaining a cow tag is far easier than getting a bull tag. In fact, cow tags may be available over the counter in some units. If you indeed draw a bull tag, you should do everything in your power to thoroughly investigate the hunt and get to the unit several days in advance in order to scout. This could be your best opportunity in a lifetime to take a trophy bull. If you aren't an experienced elk hunter and can afford it, you might consider hiring an outfitter.

Cold-weather hunting has its pitfalls. It's possible the weather could be brutal, with gale force winds, blizzards and sub-zero temperatures. You need to be prepared for every eventuality, including unseasonably warm days that could push temperatures into the 60s and 70s.

During extremely cold days, pay special attention to boots, gloves, hats and some sort of face mask or balaclava that protects your face from stinging arctic winds. Layered clothing, rather than wearing a single bulky garment, is the best way to dress.

Sub-zero temperatures require you to condition your firearm. It's not uncommon for a rifle to fail to fire; this usually happens when a sluggish or inoperative firing pin fails because the grease or oil thickens.

Before you leave for your hunt, disassemble and completely degrease your rifle. Then lubricate it with a special grease made especially for very cold temperatures (there are several on the market). If you don't want to do this yourself, take the rifle to a gun-smith. Either way, be sure to degrease your rifle. What you don't want is a gun that doesn't shoot when the bull presents the shot.

This happened to me once, on an early December elk hunt in Canada when the temperature was -25°F. Using my trustworthy .30-06 Winchester Model 70, I centered the scope on a big bull and was shocked when the rifle failed to fire. All I heard was the click of the firing pin. Frantically, I ejected the shell, and chambered another cartridge. Again the gun didn't fire. All the while the bull was standing at the edge of timber across a clearing, and was beginning to look nervous. I was nervous too, and tried for the third time. This time the rifle roared and the bull was mine. I looked at the two cartridges that failed to go off and noted a very slight indentation on the primers made by a sluggish firing pin that didn't have the force to properly strike the primer.

LATE-SEASON STRATEGIES

Since you'll likely have snow during a late hunt, tracking is an effective technique. Don't be fooled into thinking that just because you've found a red-hot track the elk is just ahead. A walking elk can outpace a human who is trotting. Prepare for a long hike, with the proper clothing and gear. You might walk much farther than you anticipated. A migrating elk may walk 10 miles or more without stopping. Animals traveling from feeding to bedding areas may walk 3 to 4 miles, sometimes more.

Snow may be noisy; in fact you can count on it if the weather is cold. Crusted snow is the worse, and will crack loudly. Snow that has warmed to just the mid-20s or 30s squeaks noisily when the temperature drops. It becomes noiser as it gets colder. Because of the noise factor, you'll have your work cut out for you to silently track late-season elk in snow. Most of the time it simply can't be done; in that case, try to set up an ambush ahead if you have any inkling where the elk are going.

Elk tend to feed longer in the early morning if the air is cold and snow is present. They can no longer simply feed by lowering their heads and nipping off forage as they do in warmer weather, but must paw through snow to expose grass. This is a time-consuming process, taking the elk longer to fill their bellies. Furthermore, the cold temperatures require them to eat enough to supply adequate calories to keep their energy level up.

This being the case, you should continue glassing for an hour or two after the sun rises. Check out small basins or pockets in out-of-way places. I like to climb as high as I can, and glass all potential feeding areas. If I spot elk in the distance and it will take a

LATE ELK SEASONS often push huge bulls from high elevations and no-hunting zones into predictable areas with relatively easy hunter access.

couple hours or more to get to them, I'll slowly work my way over; by the time I get there the elk will probably be bedded in the timber. I'll find a spot along the edge of the forest with the wind in my favor, and wait for the elk to come out to feed. Again, they'll usually be in the clearings long before sundown.

Elk often feed on open ridges where constant winds blow away the snow. They may remain in the vicinity all winter, even if snow piles high in adjacent areas. Food is always the priority that keeps them attracted to certain areas.

Don't sell elk short when it comes to severe arctic weather. They'll remain exposed, even in stiff gale winds, in order to find sufficient forage. These are tough animals that came to America from Siberia. Elk have thick skin and warm pelts, and are exceedingly rugged.

The reward of hunting the late season is finding a trophy elk located relatively close to a road. Go the extra mile if you have a late-season tag; the odds don't get any better for taking a big bull.

Trophy Hunting

If you read outdoor magazines, or look at elk hunting videos or shows on TV, you've no doubt seen smiling hunters posing next to big six-point bulls. Every hunter would love to set his sights on a bull of that stature, but some places, even in prime elk habitat, have few if any six-point elk. Some hunters believe if they hunt long and hard enough, they'll eventually find the huge bull of their dreams.

Elk antlers are the product of an animal's nutrition, genes and age. For the most part, the latter is by far the most important. If an elk doesn't live long enough, he won't grow large antlers, regardless of his ancestry or the quality of his feed. It usually takes at least 4 years for antlers to develop good mass and tine length, and a bull that's 7 to 8 years old is in his prime. In places where hunter pressure is heavy, typically on public land with good access and multiple seasons, elk are commonly harvested so consistently that a 3-year-old bull is the oldest bull on the mountain. Most of the bulls in those situations are raghorns—bulls that have worn antlers for only 2 years and have small four- or five-point racks.

Before discussing trophy elk, it's essential to define the term "trophy." To some people, any elk is a trophy, and rightly so. An animal need not wear impressive headgear for it to be considered a trophy. To other hunters, an elk taken with a bow or blackpowder rifle is a trophy because of the special challenges in getting close and using equipment inferior to modern centerfire rifles.

People who view antlers with regard to a "score" usually have certain parameters by which they judge a bull. For example, to most elk hunters, a bull that scores 300 Boone and Crockett points is a worthwhile objective, and one the hunter would be proud to own. Other hunters may view a trophy bull as one approaching 330 or even 350 B&C points. A small handful of hunters think nothing less than 375 B&C points is worthy of trophy status. That score is minimum for the typical category in the prestigious Boone and Crockett record book, and, on average, only about a dozen or so elk larger than 375 B&C points are taken annually.

For the purposes of this section, a trophy is defined as an outstanding bull, one judged by the dimensions of its antlers rather than the circumstances of the hunt or the equipment used. What I'm defining is an older bull, old because he has managed to survive several hunting seasons. He's probably accomplished this because he lives in a backcountry region where he easily avoided hunters simply because of the enormity and remoteness of his environment. Another possibility is that he lives on a property or hunting unit where hunter numbers are restricted, allowing the harvest of only a small portion of the bulls.

STRATEGIES FOR TROPHY ELK

There are several ways that you can pursue trophy bulls, depending on your physical capabilities, your luck at drawing limited-entry tags and your bank account. As mentioned elsewhere in this book, you can hire outfitters, hunt very expensive ranches or Indian reservations, or head for the backcountry on your own.

Because the trophy elk you seek is an older animal, you can usually count on it being a cut above the others in the intelligence department. This means you must hunt smarter and harder. Hunting the rut isn't always the answer, though some people believe big bulls are more vulnerable this time of year. Most big herd bulls keep their distance and even retreat with their cows from a call.

The later seasons are often considered prime time for big bulls, because the deep snow moves them to lower elevations where they're more accessible. Bulls often herd together in bachelor groups this time of year, offering a choice if a hunter can get within shooting distance. On the downside is the usual bad weather occurring this time of year, making hunting conditions miserable, if not inhospitable. In some cases, elk descend to lower elevations and reside on private lands where they're unavailable to hunters unless hunters lease those lands or hire an outfitter.

One of the biggest problems in trophy hunting is the very basic need to determine whether a bull is indeed of trophy status in the first place. Many people, including so-called experienced guides, cannot accurately field-judge an elk that's either moving, at a distance or in partial cover. In fact, I've been in the company of some guides who couldn't evaluate a big bull if it stood in the open 50 yards away. In the mind's eye of most people, a big elk is just that—a big elk. They have no idea how to quickly and accurately size up the antlers.

Obviously, the most skilled individuals at evaluating antlers are those who see plenty of big elk, but that luxury is not afforded to most hunters, outfitters or guides. There are, however, some field evaluation techniques that can help you make a fairly accurate call. A quick look at the royals, which are the fourth points back, gives you an idea as to the bull's worth. If those tines are exceptionally long, at least 18 inches or better, the animal has serious merit as a trophy. Long tines elsewhere are another asset, as is mass of

TROPHY BULLS, like this animal from the Sunlight Basin area near Cody, Wyoming, are the subject of many hunters' dreams. Wyoming resident Merwin Martin took this bull, which measures 417⅜ Boone and Crockett points, in mid-November of 1991. It is the biggest bull to be shot in Wyoming in more than a century.

the beams and their width. A very good bull has beams 48 to 50 inches long, with long tines. To really fine-tune the bull's antlers, have a look at the third points. They're usually the weakest, but a truly good bull has long third points as well as long tines along the entire beam. If you see a giant bull, you won't need to check these features closely. Trust me—your heart will skip a beat as you shoulder your rifle and concentrate on making a good shot.

LOCATING TROPHY ELK

So where do you find the biggest bulls in the land? Every state has its share of huge elk, but consistently the top state is Arizona. Big elk are taken not only on the famous Indian reservations there, but in national forests where the public can hunt free. Biologists claim Arizona's bulls get large because the winters are mild, allowing good antler growth in

Royal points

JUDGING TROPHIES in the field takes practice. On the bull above, however, the long and massive royals are a quick give-away that this bull is a definite "shooter."

the spring and early summer. Furthermore, the restrictive hunting seasons allow many bulls to live to ripe old age.

There's another reason; it's controversial and not widely accepted by all the people who profess to know about Arizona elk, but very definitely accepted by some, including me. Textbooks claim the last elk of the Merriam's subspecies was killed in Arizona in 1904. The Merriam's was one of six subspecies of elk in North America, and was reputed to have large antlers.

I find it curious that someone declared the Merriam's to be extinct in a vast area of the Southwest that was heavily timbered and unroaded, especially since there were no procedures to inventory or census elk. In 1904, all one could do was to ride horseback or hike.

Within the next 2 decades, elk were reintroduced to Arizona from Wyoming herds in Yellowstone National Park and from the National Elk Refuge near Jackson. To follow this theory, one must assume some of the Merriam's elk were indeed still alive, and

bred with the Yellowstone elk. If this is true, then it becomes abundantly clear that as the result of these crosses, bulls with above-average racks could be produced.

Other places to find trophies are near national parks where elk are not hunted and live many years. Many of these elk migrate out of the parks, and become available to hunters who have late-season tags. Wyoming and Montana, for example, offer late hunts for migrating Yellowstone National Park bulls.

The Wyoming hunt is held in units west of Cody and the park boundary, chiefly in the Shoshone National Forest. Lucky hunters who draw tags count on deep snow driving elk out of Yellowstone and the adjacent national forest high country and down to lower elevations.

I live within a few hundred yards of the forest boundary, and have observed this migration phenom-enon for years. My wife took a very big bull almost within a stone's throw of our house. She'd drawn a late tag and killed the bull in early December. I'm convinced the bull lived most of the year in or around the Yellowstone backcountry, and showed up near our home when the heavy snow up high evicted him and all the other elk. Prior to the migration, you'd do well to see an elk within 3 miles of the highway, but once the migration occurs, you can virtually see elk from the roads.

Montana has the premier late trophy hunt in the Gallatin National Forest just outside Gardiner, which is the north gate of Yellowstone. Elk make an exodus from the park and head to winter ranges in lower elevations, both on public land and ranchland. The state has special 4-day hunts for bulls. These mini-seasons begin in December and run into February. When the winters are normal, huge bulls are taken by hunters who draw tags, and most of the bulls are taken on public land fairly close to roads.

I've never drawn a tag here, though I've tried for years. I've gone along as an observer, accompanying a number of hunters, and have witnessed many trophies taken. This is perhaps the finest trophy elk hunt on public land in the country.

Colorado has late hunts for elk exiting Rocky Mountain National Park. This is also a migration hunt where hunters must draw a tag in a lottery.

In Canada, enormous bulls leaving Jasper and Banff National Parks are hunted on adjacent public lands. Canada has "crown lands" similar to our national forests. Americans can't hunt here unguided, and must hire an outfitter.

I've made two trips to Canada's big-bull country. One was late in the season, and the other during the bugling period.

The late hunt was in December, which was the last week of the regular season. It was bitterly cold, with the temperature well below zero every night as well as every day. My outfitters, Mike and Pat Bates, had a comfortable tent camp set up a few miles from the nearest road, and we hunted at least 15 miles away from camp every day on horseback, sometimes much farther.

We concentrated our efforts outside Banff National Park where Clarence Brown took, at that time, the

The author with a trophy bull from Utah

third biggest bull in the world. Our efforts for the first 5 days were in vain, but miraculously, a trio of big bulls showed up on the last afternoon. My partner had first shot and downed a huge bull that scored 362 Boone and Crockett points, winning that year's Bull of the Woods contest sponsored by the Rocky Mountain Elk Foundation. I shot the next biggest bull, a dandy seven-by-seven that I was very proud to tag.

Those trophies didn't come easy. We hunted in places during gale-force blizzards that could have killed us. One day we rode so so many miles I couldn't believe it, and I was half frozen in the saddle most of the time. We figured we rode 40 miles that day, starting from camp at 4 A.M. and returning at 10 P.M. It was Thanksgiving Day, and we were too tired to eat the traditional turkey and fixings for dinner when we finally got back to camp.

The September hunt wasn't nearly as eventful. We were hunting resident rather than migratory elk, and had plenty of company from other hunters, far more than I expected. Even so, my partner took a nice six-point bull that we located about 5 miles from camp.

It's easy to check areas in states that have trophy bulls by simply looking through the statistics in the Boone and Crockett record book. Each trophy is listed, along with when and where it was taken. Be sure to consider only those elk taken in recent years, because elk populations and quality potential have changed enormously with the passage of time. For example, the Plute bull, which was the world record elk until it was displaced in 1998, was taken in Dark Canyon, Colorado, around 1899. Looking for a bull like it in Dark Canyon today wouldn't be very prudent—a waste of time.

The bottom line in looking for a trophy bull—no matter how you define it—is to do research on whether such bulls exist in the area you plan on hunting. Obviously, you can't shoot a trophy bull if he doesn't live there. And remember, a trophy bull is an old bull, so go where there are fewer hunters. Bulls need to survive a handful of hunting seasons to grow trophy antlers.

After the Shot

The smile on your face when your elk goes down may quickly turn into a frown if you haven't already formulated a plan to get the animal out of the woods. Your prize is enormous compared to a deer, with mature bulls commonly weighing up to 800 pounds, cows 450 or more.

Unfortunately, many hunters are woefully unprepared to accomplish the herculean chore of moving this much meat. Many hunters are optimists, making the assumption that somehow they'll get the job done, if and when they put an elk to the ground.

The optimism fades when reality sets in and you stare in amazement at the huge animal lying on the ground a mile from the road, and most of it uphill. A major ordeal awaits, and now is the time that your planning should take effect.

First you'll probably want to take photos of your prize, but do so only after the animal is properly tagged. Be quick with your photos, since you're now racing with time. As soon as the elk expires, bacteria immediately go to work in its body. Your primary and sole objective is to remove the innards without delay since you must cool the carcass quickly.

FIELD-DRESSING, SKINNING AND QUARTERING

Field-dressing a deer is child's play when compared to an elk. The innards of an elk may weigh as much as an entire deer. It might be difficult, if not almost impossible, to position the elk for dressing if you're

alone and it's wedged into some brush on a steep slope with the belly facing the ground. It might be necessary to chop away brush in order to roll the animal. A small saw comes in handy, and ropes will help you maneuver the carcass and hold it firmly on a steep incline.

If you quarter or bone the elk, skinning the carcass is required in most cases. Skinning also helps eliminate body heat, aiding in cooling the carcass. The field-dressing, skinning, and boning or quartering work is best learned by watching an experienced person do it. If you haven't been able to witness the task, rent one of the many videos on the subject. It's far easier to learn from a video than a book. Be aware that state laws may require you to leave evidence of sex attached to the carcass. To do so, it's easiest to simply allow the testicular sac on a bull and the udders on a cow to remain intact. Most states require them to remain attached until the meat arrives at your home or at the processing plant.

Essentially, field-dressing an elk is the same as doing so to a deer, except you'll be working with far more weight and mass. The only extra equipment you'll need is a small saw to cut bone and branches, and ropes to help tie the legs so you can work at dressing. Of course, a good knife and a knife sharpener are essential for any operation.

If you must leave the carcass, quarters or boned meat overnight or for several hours in order to round up your pals or a couple horses, place the meat in a shady area and lay it on several branches that allow air to circulate underneath. Place some boughs on top to hide the meat from predators—the feathered, furred and human types. It doesn't happen often, but thieves have been known to steal an elk. If you're hunting in grizzly bear country, special laws may apply. You'll probably be required to hang the meat 10 feet off the ground to thwart raiding grizzlies. This is no easy task, as you can imagine. Be sure to check the regs

SPECIALTY KNIVES, such as this model from Knives of Alaska, have a curved blade and a gut hook for easy field-dressing and skinning.

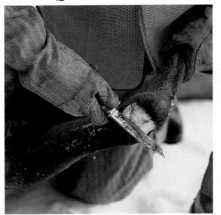

BEND a leg sharply, then cut the skin around the joint to remove the lower leg. Repeat on all legs.

SAW off the head after skinning the neck area. Sawing it before skinning would force hair into the meat.

CUT between the third and fourth ribs, from the backbone to the tips of the ribs. Cut from inside the body.

SEPARATE the front half of the animal from the rear half by sawing through the backbone.

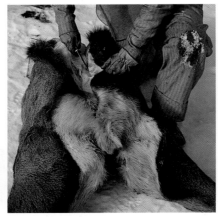

SPLIT the hide along the backbone on both halves, then peel it back several inches on each side of the cut.

PROP one half against your legs, then begin sawing lengthwise through the backbone.

CONTINUE cutting while keeping the back off the ground. Gravity will help pull the quarters apart, making the cutting easier. Your saw will not bind, as it would if the half were lying on the ground.

A QUARTERED elk looks like this. Depending on the animal's size, elk quarters weigh 60 to 125 pounds each. Where the law allows, some hunters bone the animal in the field to reduce weight.

DRAG out a hindquarter by punching a hole behind the last rib, then threading a rope through and tying as pictured. This way, you drag with the grain of the hair. To drag out a forequarter, tie a rope tightly around the neck.

before your hunt so you can be prepared with the proper gear. The only way to hang that much meat 10 feet high is to quarter or bone the carcass and raise it with a small portable pulley system. This regulation is in effect only if you leave the elk overnight. If it's impossible to raise it, wildlife officers recommend you move the meat to the center of an opening. When you return for it later you'll be able to observe it from a distance to see if a grizzly is feeding on it, or if a bear has been present. Most grizzly-human confrontations occur when the bear discovers the elk and starts feeding on it. If that happens, remember the elk belongs to the grizzly. A game warden may or may not reissue you another tag.

Before leaving the elk to get help, be sure you can find it again. Mark the location with a GPS unit if you have one, or flag a trail out with orange or red ribbon or surveyor's tape. Be sure you remove the ribbon when you leave with the elk.

If you shoot an elk in the waning hours of shooting light, you probably won't be able to get it out that evening unless it falls close to a road or trail and you can return quickly with some pals. You might find yourself in a big hurry because of the impending darkness, but pay attention to details such as thorough field-dressing and marking the spot as well as the trail out. You'll be glad when you return the next day.

GETTING YOUR ELK OUT OF THE WOODS

You can transport an elk by using horses or your back. The latter is obviously the toughest, and could be the most memorable aspect of your hunt, especially if you hurt yourself in the process. Don't take on more of a load than you can handle. A quarter of a mature bull weighs between 80 to 100 pounds or more, which is a heavy burden to carry over rough terrain. And remember, there are four quarters, and the antlers, cape, and your gear as well. A sturdy pack frame that fits well helps reduce the discomfort of carrying the weight.

Before you begin carrying the meat, be sure you've investigated every possible route, since you want to make the chore as easy on yourself as possible. Check out the trails and contours of the land. If you must hike up a steep hill, it might be easier to walk on the level for an extra half mile and then top out through a saddle rather than take the shortest straight uphill route. Rest frequently, and travel at a comfortable pace. When carrying antlers, it's a good idea to tie plenty of orange flagging on them so you don't attract another hunter's unwanted attention.

Horses make the job a whole lot easier, but be aware it takes two horses (or mules) to pack one elk. A

dead-weight load of 200 to 250 pounds is about maximum for a horse. Dead weight is much different than the weight of a person riding a horse. Dead weight just sits there, but a human moves in the saddle, typically far forward when going up steep hills, and back in the saddle when going down. It's called "being alive in the saddle." This helps the horse considerably to balance the weight.

If you don't have horses, you can often rent them from guest ranches or others who advertise in local papers. You might try contacting the local chamber of commerce for a list of rental horses. Never rent horses unless you or someone in your party is thoroughly acquainted with horses and packing. You must be familiar with the appropriate tack, knots, and horses in general. It's also necessary to determine if the horses have packed game before. If not, you might have a rodeo on your hands, ending up with some horses or people getting hurt. Most horses must be trained to carry meat.

In some towns you can hire a wrangler or packer to bring out your elk. The cost usually depends on how far he must go to retrieve the animal, but will likely range from $100 to $250. Make arrangements with a packer before you hunt, so if you need his services he'll be available.

Be aware that in popular hunting towns, packers may be busy with several elk to haul out. It's a good idea to line up two or three, so one is ready to go when you need him. To find a packer, inquire with the chamber of commerce, or people who own guest ranches. The latter are apt to know most people in town who have horses. You might also ask local outfitters, game wardens and ranchers.

Another option, and one I like best if no horses are available, is to roll the meat out on a wheeled carrier. A wheel is one of civilization's greatest inventions, and it simplifies the task of transporting a heavy load. You can make a carrier yourself or buy a commercial model. The best types are those with one wheel, not two, since the extra wheel easily becomes entangled in brush and makes the device difficult to roll on uneven terrain. Handles on each end allow two people to roll it, and brakes are a good idea. Be aware that any kind of wheeled unit is illegal in wilderness areas, but few hunters hike in to those backcountry areas; most ride in on horses.

A sturdy carrier works in amazing places. My wife shot a bull moose in a swamp, and together we were able to wheel chunks of it it through willow patches, stony creeks and mucky spots. Another time I killed a blacktail buck in a clearcut area in western Washington 2 miles from my truck. The wheeled carrier got it out nicely, bouncing through and across

Skinning and Boning an Elk

If you don't want to quarter the meat with a saw, but want to bone it or cut the quarters off at the joints, you'll need to skin the carcass. In this instance the elk doesn't have to be field-dressed.

Start the skinning process by making the same belly cut as if you were going to field-dress, but don't penetrate inside to the cavity. Start the cut at the anus area and continue to the throat, unless you intend to cape the carcass. Next, cut around each knee joint with your knife. On the back or hind end, start another cut from the knee up to the belly cut, working on the underside of each leg. Do the same in the front, working from the knee to the brisket, again working underneath.

Now you can start skinning. Start at any point, and continue to work until the entire top half is skinned, including the rear and front legs. Here's the beauty of this quartering system because it doesn't require a saw. Pull on the back leg and you'll see where it moves back and forth. Using a sharp knife, make a deep cut next to the pelvic bone and work around it. Move the leg every now and then to see where the joint connects it to the body. Cut to that joint, and by working your knife point into the middle of the joint, you can easily sever it from the body. Lay the quarter in the shade on a clean surface, or better yet, place it in a meat bag and hang it in the shade.

The front quarter is also cut off with a knife, but the joint is different. Start cutting where the leg joins the body and work your way around the shoulder. Again, move the leg back and forth so you can see where it's connected to the joint. This joint is farther up toward the spine than you'll expect, but keep lifting and cutting around the shoulder and you'll easily cut through it.

When you're done you'll have both quarters removed. Of course, the bones are in them, and these are the only bones you'll have to deal with. Now you must remove the rest of the meat on the skinned side of the carcass. Cut away the backstrap that lies along the spine, and slice away the flank meat covering the ribs. More meat in the neck region needs to be cut away. If you want the meat between the ribs, which is delicious, carefully strip it off, but don't puncture the cavity. Make sure you're aware of your state laws regarding waste of game meat, so you know what you must take out.

The tenderloins lie inside the body, which presents a seemingly puzzling situation. How to get at them if you haven't field-dressed the animal? This is a simple operation, but to do it you must know where the tenderloins lie. It's best to watch someone do this before you try it. You'll note that the ribs stop about three-fourths of the way back and don't continue all the way to the rear. Just behind the last rib, reach your fingers in just under the spine and feel for the loins. The paunch may be tight, pressing upward, but you can generally insert your fingers and a knife and carefully strip out the tenderloin.

Now examine the carcass and keep cutting away chunks of meat along the flanks and the pelvic and neck regions, until you have it all. With this side of the animal boned, you're ready to flip it and work the other side. Using a rope or sheer energy, grab one of the legs underneath and roll the elk over. Repeat the procedure until that side is also boned.

When you're done, you'll have a completely boned-out carcass lying on the ground, minus the legs. You won't waste any more meat than you would if you cut the elk up at a sanitary meat processing house with all the tools and equipment.

To bone the carcass without taking any leg bones, do the same as above, but trim all the meat off the legs. You don't need to remove the legs at the joints, and can keep them connected at the joints if you wish. By completely boning the entire carcass you'll be able to leave behind much weight, and you can carry the boned meat in a rucksack or large backpack, making as many trips as required.

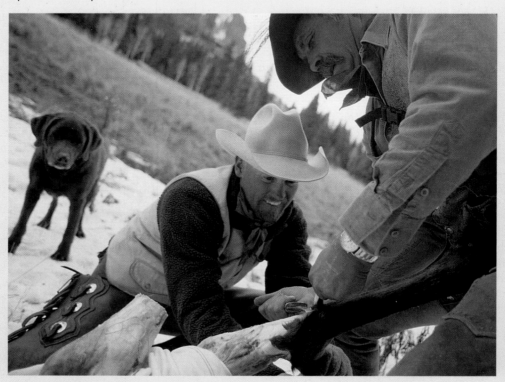

Guides skinning an elk

PLAN your route carefully before beginning to pack out an elk. The last thing you want is to be faced with backtracking or climbing a steep hill with a full load on your back.

stumps, downed logs and thick debris. I can't remember how many elk I've transported with it.

Another possible way to move your elk is the two-man pole carry. Find a sturdy, lightweight pole in the forest, and attach the meat in the middle with ropes, insuring that the meat can't swing around as it's being carried, thus unbalancing the carriers. Place some sort of pad, such as a shirt or jacket, on your shoulder to help ease the load. I first started using the pole system with mule deer in Utah and hadn't considered it as a means to haul elk until a hunt where my pal and I were faced with a 3-mile carry. The elk lay on an aspen slope, requiring a carry across two steep draws. Using my meat saw, I cut a dead but very sound aspen about 8 feet long and 4 inches in diameter. We lashed a pair of front quarters firmly to the pole and made a reasonably easy trek to the truck. We returned, carried out the hindquarters, and made a final trip with the neck, cape, antlers and

gear. It was after dark when we were done, but at least the chore was accomplished in a day. We didn't want to leave the meat overnight in that instance because of the large numbers of black bears in the area.

Most deer hunters drag a deer out of the woods. Don't even think about doing this with a whole elk, unless you can go straight downhill with no level spots or inclines along your route. Snow makes dragging easier. There are plastic or fabric sleds that roll up in a compact unit, made especially for dragging a heavy object. Shaped like a rectangular sheet with pull ropes and grommets to tie ropes to, they make dragging a great deal easier. I've only seen sleds that accommodate deer, but you can lash two quarters of an elk and drag.

If you use an ATV, be sure to obey all rules, whether it's private or public ground. There's a great temptation to drive to a downed elk, thus eliminating a whole lot of strain and pain, but be sure you're within the law and the landowner's wishes.

Don't make the mistake of taking the task of transporting your elk out lightly. This is a major part of the hunt, and to do it successfully you must be well prepared.

GETTING YOUR ELK HOME

Once your elk is transported from the woods and loaded in a vehicle, you have several options. If you live nearby, you can take it home and butcher it yourself, or take it to a local meat processor. If you're a nonresident, you'll obviously need to choose a means of getting it home, and that depends on whether you've flown or driven a vehicle to the hunt.

In the event that you've flown, you can take the meat with you on the airplane, or have a processor ship it to you after it's been cut up and wrapped. In the latter case, be sure you advise the processor specifically how you want the meat cut up. For example, you might like several roasts, or few or no roasts; you might prefer ground meat to stew meat, etc. You also should specify how large your family is and how many pieces of meat you want per package. For example, you might want only two steaks per package, or more. Be sure to indicate how much ground meat you want in a package. If you request 1½-pound packages, you'll get five or six burgers out of it. A 1-pound package gives you about four burgers. You also need to specify how much suet you'd like with your ground meat. Lean meat usually amounts to 10 percent or less suet, which means 1 pound of suet for 10 pounds of meat. You can also choose between beef or pork suet or a mixture of both.

Ask the processor to be specific as to the contents of each package. For example, the tenderloins are the choice cuts, and you don't want them labeled simply as "steaks." Roasts should be identified accordingly, such as "shoulder roast," "rump roast," etc. Also, be sure the word "elk" is written on the package, as well as the date. You don't want to confuse an elk roast with a deer roast, and if you're fortunate enough to have gone on two elk hunts 2 years in a row, you'll probably want to eat the older meat first. The more information on the package, the easier it will be to cook it correctly. Elk meat is too good to be cooked improperly.

It's a good idea to compare processing prices before you commit the elk carcass. I know of two processors in the same town, both of whom have good reputations, that charge as much as 30 cents a pound difference in their rates. The price you pay is "hanging weight." Say each quarter weighs 100 pounds

and the rate is 50 cents per pound. At 400 pounds, you'll pay $200, which doesn't include shipping.

Be aware that shipping costs are fairly high, since the meat must undoubtedly be flown and not sent by truck. Assume you want to ship 60 pounds of packaged meat from each quarter, and it costs $2 per pound to ship. You're looking at 240 pounds of meat, amounting to $480 to ship it. You can cut the shipping costs somewhat by flying the meat "second-day air" instead of "next-day air."

There might be additional costs. Some processors could charge extra to bone the quarters, and if you've brought the whole carcass in unskinned, or the quarters unskinned, you could be charged extra for skinning.

Many hunters also like sausage, salami, frankfurters and jerky made from their meat. You'll pay extra for these, even though it's your meat (but maybe not). State laws forbid the sale of wild game; essentially you're paying for the processor's labor, suet, sausage casings and spices. Expect to pay at least $1 per pound for this meat, depending on what kind you're buying, and don't count on getting the meat from your own animal. Many processors put the meat from several animals in a big vat and make large batches of sausages. It's conceivable the sausage you get could be made from someone else's elk, or even deer or antelope. Sausage being what it is, it all tastes similar. If you want your own meat, be sure you tell the processor.

Check out the processors in the area before you hunt and find out their procedures and costs. You could save a lot of money and hassle by doing some preliminary investigation.

You can fly your meat home with you, and then take it to a local processor where you live or cut it up yourself. The most inexpensive way to fly with meat is to bone it, chill it, put it in coolers, take it as excess baggage, and cut it up yourself when you get home. Most airlines allow you to check two bags; everything over that is charged an excess baggage fee, which is about $50. Typically you'll have a rifle in a case, and at least one large duffel bag, so you're looking at excess costs.

Most, if not all, airlines have a maximum weight limitation of 70 pounds per container. I like to thoroughly chill the meat and put it in coolers that I buy in the town where I hunt. By the time I get home, I can cut the meat up, package it and freeze it. It's not a good idea to freeze the meat in large chunks, incidentally, because then you'll have to thaw it to cut it up, and then freeze it again. If thoroughly chilled, meat usually stays cold in an insulated cooler for at least 24 hours. You can keep it cooler by adding several packages of the so-called "blue ice" that you can buy at department stores. This is usually a gel that freezes hard and stays cold for longer periods than regular ice. Another advantage is it doesn't thaw and leak, though I've found some that flimsy packages that indeed did leak gel. To be on the safe side, I put each package in a Ziploc bag.

If you ship frozen meat and want to put dry ice in the container, be sure you alert the airline agent when you check your baggage. Better yet, call in advance and check with the airline. Dry ice is a restricted item and may or may not be allowed.

If you've driven to your hunt and want to bring the meat home in your vehicle, you can wrap quarters in old quilts or sleeping bags. Be sure the quarters are well chilled before you wrap them. Keep them tightly covered during the day, and if you stop at night at a highway rest area or motel and the evening air is cool, loosen the wrapping and allow the cold air to circulate.

If you've had the meat processed, packaged and frozen, put it in coolers or insulated boxes (if the processor has them), and put some dry ice on top. The cool air from the dry ice descends. Never put dry ice on the bottom. You can buy dry ice at some grocery stores, or from meat processors. It's very expensive, and you should calculate how much you need to get home.

If you cut and wrap the meat yourself, there are procedures to keep it in a high-quality state for long periods. I've often read that frozen wild game has a shelf life in the freezer of no more than a year. I don't believe it. With proper packaging, I've found 3-year-old meat tasty and in good condition.

The very best way to package meat is to use a vacuum sealer, which sucks out all the air. These cost around $300, and most folks don't use them. The enemy of any frozen meat is "freezer burn," which

occurs when air comes in contact with the meat, even air in the package itself. Meat that is freezer burned is edible, but it looks, smells and tastes a bit gamey.

I start off by tightly wrapping the meat in a good quality plastic wrap. Squeeze out all the air while you work, and tape it securely. Next, wrap it in special freezer wrap, again squeezing out all the air. Tape it and label it accordingly.

Elk hunting is more than bringing home an animal, and when you do, it's a special bonus. You'll smile all the way through dinner. Elk meat is simply wonderful, as long as it's processed and stored correctly.

Common Elk-Hunting Errors

On average, only 20 percent of all elk hunters take home an elk each year. Here are some of the reasons why that's so:

•*Reliance on vehicles.* If the truth were known, the majority of hunters don't get very far away from their pickup truck, SUV or ATV. Many people hunt close to roads because they either don't understand elk behavior, or are unwilling to put in the effort to go to the elk. That, more often than not, means hiking up slopes, and usually through timber, rocks, brush and other obstacles. Many forest roads and trails allow standard vehicles and ATVs. Hunters believe all they need to do is drive the back roads, spot an elk and shoot it. That's the rare exception, because elk are aware of places frequented by people and shun them.

•*Failure to penetrate the forest.* This differs from the above in that many people hike around in the woods, genuinely believing they're hunting correctly, but in reality they aren't getting far enough in the back-country. Elk often take refuge a long way from a road, and only those hunters willing to put in the extra mile or two find them. There are three main reasons why people don't get very far from roads. The first and most basic is being out of shape, and finding it difficult and perhaps painful to get around in steep terrain. High altitudes compound the problem by making it even more physically uncomfort-

able. Secondly, some hunters purposely stay close to roads for logistic reasons—if they get an elk they want to be assured they can get it out without a major ordeal. And last, some people are afraid of getting lost and are unwilling to travel very far into the woods.

•*Watching meadows in the daytime.* Some folks erroneously believe elk feed in meadows on and off during the entire day. That's almost never the case, especially if there's any sort of hunting pressure. This is a large waste of time; it would be far better to sit in the woods near a trail where elk might be pushed toward you by other hunters.

•*Not understanding elk behavior.* Hunters who are unfamiliar with elk don't know their habits and therefore have no idea how, where and when to hunt them. Strategies depend on understanding the quarry. The more you know about them the better.

•*No knowledge of elk communication.* It's important to know how to talk to elk, not only during the bugling season, but for the rest of the fall when elk routinely vocalize. Cow calls work year-round, and should be used as the situation demands.

•*Not hunting early and late enough in the day.* Elk are most active during the night. They begin moving from their bedding areas to feeding areas close to sundown or just afterward, and head back to bedding areas around sunrise. Hunters must be in the woods long before legal shooting hours arrive, and stay until shooting hours are over.

•*Inability to see elk.* Because elk are large animals, many hunters expect them to be conspicuous. That's often not the case, since they blend in well with their surroundings. Binoculars must be used continually, especially early and late in the day.

PROPER PHYSICAL CONDITIONING allows you to hunt hard from dark to dark. Get in shape before the hunt so you can spend more time hunting and less time resting.

The Future of Elk Hunting

The first elk restocking efforts were not without controversy. In fact, many of the early projects were dismal failures. But enough elk survived the long treks and rough handling during the primitive trapping efforts to restore the species in both historic and new ranges.

The big question surrounding the future of any wildlife species is mankind's ability to maintain adequate habitat. Make no mistake—it is humans who destroy it and only humans can preserve it. Without all the tenets of a sound environment, no species can thrive. It appears the habitat for elk is adequately protected, due in large part to the efforts of the Rocky Mountain Elk Foundation. This organization, established in 1984 in Troy, Montana, has raised countless millions of dollars to protect and preserve critical lands used by elk. More than 100,000 dedicated members flock to more than 500 fundraising chapter banquets around the country each year to support elk-habitat programs.

While it's comfortable to know that elk numbers are increasing every year, there's always the nagging question of our legal ability to hunt elk. Without question, the elk populations are strong enough to sustain hunting. Some states even allow hunters to harvest two elk, the second one being antlerless. This is due to large herds that must be trimmed every year to insure the animals won't exceed the land's ability to support them.

Despite these burgeoning populations, there are individuals and groups that would like to see all hunting terminated, regardless of the inhumane effects of starvation and disease caused by too many animals. Concerned pro-hunters point to some species that have already been placed on the no-hunting list despite their abundance, such as mountain lions in California. By a ballot box vote, citizens of that state decided to end lion hunting. In Colorado, Oregon and Washington, spring bear hunting was ended by public votes.

Comparing elk with bears and lions, however, is like comparing apples and oranges. The public has always had romantic notions about predators, both winged and furred. Elk, on the other hand, can cause tremendous damage to crops, fences and property, and most observers believe these animals must be harvested to keep them in balance with the habitat's carrying capacity.

Of more concern is the increasing age of the average hunter. This reflects the sobering fact that fewer youngsters are hunting today than in the past. Obviously, the tradition of hunting cannot be maintained if the sport isn't passed on from one generation to the next. This shortcoming is recognized by the hunting community as a serious problem, and more youth programs are in place these days to introduce kids to hunting and the outdoors.

Statistics also indicate that more women are hunting nowadays than in the past, which is great news, since many animal-rights groups perceive hunting as a macho sport. Female hunters dispel this notion and give the correct impression that hunting is a wholesome activity regardless of gender.

I believe elk and elk hunting will be around for a long time to come. And as long as hunting is allowed to continue, elk will be the beloved quarry of hundreds of thousands of sportsmen and women each year.

Rocky Mountain Elk Foundation

The mission of the Rocky Mountain Elk Foundation (RMEF) is to ensure the future of elk, other wildlife and their habitat. In support of this mission, the RMEF is committed to:

• Conserving, restoring and enhancing natural habitats;
• Promoting the sound management of wild, free-ranging elk, which may be hunted or otherwise enjoyed;
• Fostering cooperation among federal, state and private organizations and individuals in wildlife management and habitat conservation; and
• Educating RMEF members and the public about habitat conservation, the value of hunting, hunting ethics and wildlife management.

Since 1984, the RMEF has funded more than 2,700 conservation projects in 48 states and 8 Canadian provinces. In total, the RMEF has conserved and enhanced over 3,000,000 acres of wildlife habitat. For information on becoming a member, write to: Rocky Mountain Elk Foundation, P.O. Box 8249, Missoula, MT 59807-8249; or check them out at **www.elkfoundation.org** on the Internet. As a member, you'll get to enjoy the RMEF bi-monthly magazine, *Bugle,* which is packed with informative and entertaining articles. I'm proud to say I've been on board with the RMEF since day one, and I invite you to join me in supporting the future of the elk.

Index

Creative Publishing international, Inc.
offers a variety of how-to books.
For information write:
  Creative Publishing international, Inc.
  Subscriber Books
  5900 Green Oak Drive
  Minnetonka, MN 55343

Contributing Photographers (Note: T=*Top*, C=*Center*, B=*Bottom*, L=*Left*, R=*Right*, i=*Inset*)

Toby Bridges
Pearl, IL
© *Toby Bridges: p. 40*

Tim Christie
timchristie.com
© *Tim Christie: pp. 15, 16-17, 24-25, 26 both, 32-33, 53, 67, 70, 71, 72, 74-75, 76L, 76C, 79, 82, 88-89, 91TR, 102, 119*

Cherie Cincilla
Outdoor Life magazine
© *Cherie Cincilla/Outdoor Life: p. 118*

Michael H. Francis
Billings, MT
© *Micheal H. Francis: pp. 10, 13TL, 13TR, 28-29, 29B, 77R, 109*

The Green Agency
www.greenagency.net
© *Bill Buckley: back cover-CR, pp. 39, 56-57, 62-63, 64 both, 68-69, 77L, 86, 92T, 114*
© *Rich Kirchner: p. 9B*
© *Stan Osolinski: p. 13BR*
© *Bill Vaznis: p. 43*

Donald M. Jones
Troy, MT
© *Donald M. Jones: cover, back cover-TR, pp. 6-7, 12, 14B, 22, 25R, 27 all, 45B, 61, 77C, 77i, 92B, 95, 99, 100, 106-107, 122*

Mark Kayser
Pierre, SD
© *Mark Kayser: back cover-BR, pp. 14T, 59, 80-81*

Stephen W. Maas
Wyoming, MN
© *Stephen W. Maas: pp. 4-5, 8-9, 11, 35, 84 both, 112*

Bill McRae
Coteau, WY
© *Bill McRae: pp. 48, 104*

Mark Raycroft
Trenton, Ontario, Canada
© *Mark Raycroft: pp. 18, 96*

Tom Stack & Associates
Key Largo, FL
© *Greg Vaughn: p. 9T*

Sil Strung
Bozeman, MT
© *Sil Strung: p. 116 all*

Tom Walker
Denali Park, AK
© *Tom Walker: pp. 20-21, 76R*

Jim Zumbo
Cody, WY
© *Jim Zumbo: back cover-TL, pp. 34, 111, 113*

Contributing Illustrator

Cynthie Fisher
Hamilton, MT
© *Cynthie Fisher: pp. 19, 35*

Creative Publishing international is the most complete source of How-To Information for the Outdoorsman

THE COMPLETE HUNTER™ *Series*

- *Whitetail Deer*
- *Dressing & Cooking Wild Game*
- *Advanced Whitetail Hunting*
- *Bowhunting Equipment & Skills*
- *Understanding Whitetails*
- *Venison Cookery*
- *Muzzleloading*
- *Wild Turkey*
- *Duck Hunting*
- *America's Favorite Wild Game Recipes*
- *Upland Game Birds*
- *The Complete Guide to Hunting*
- *Game Bird Cookery*
- *North American Game Birds*
- *North American Game Animals*
- *Elk Hunting*

The Freshwater Angler™ *Series*

- *Largemouth Bass*
- *The New Cleaning & Cooking Fish*
- *Fishing Tips & Tricks*
- *Trout*
- *Panfish*
- *All-Time Favorite Fish Recipes*
- *Fishing for Catfish*
- *Fishing With Artificial Lures*
- *Successful Walleye Fishing*
- *Advanced Bass Fishing*
- *The Art of Fly Tying*
- *The Art of Freshwater Fishing*
- *Fishing Rivers & Streams*
- *Northern Pike & Muskie*
- *Freshwater Gamefish of North America*
- *Fishing With Live Bait*
- *Fly Fishing for Trout in Streams*
- *Smallmouth Bass*
- *Modern Methods of Ice Fishing*

The Complete FLY FISHERMAN™ *Series*

- *Fly-Tying Techniques & Patterns*
- *Fly-Fishing Equipment & Skills*
- *Fishing Nymphs, Wet Flies & Streamers – Subsurface Techniques for Trout in Streams*
- *Fishing Dry Flies – Surface Presentations for Trout in Streams*

FOR A LIST OF PARTICIPATING RETAILERS
NEAR YOU, CALL 1-800-328-0590